Investing in a
Secular Bear Market

Investing in a Secular Bear Market

Michael A. Alexander

iUniverse, Inc.
New York Lincoln Shanghai

Investing in a Secular Bear Market

iUniverse books may be ordered through booksellers or by contacting:

iUniverse
2021 Pine Lake Road, Suite 100
Lincoln, NE 68512
www.iuniverse.com
1-800-Authors (1-800-288-4677)

ISBN: 0-595-34206-X

Printed in the United States of America

Contents

List of Tables

List of Figures

Preface to Paperback Edition

This book was originally published in hardcover by 21st Century Investors with the title *Retiring Rich* in 2003. Two years have elapsed since original publication, enough time to give a preliminary assessment on the forecasts made. The basic cycle analysis has been quite accurate with respect to the stock market, as represented by the S&P500. The forecast of the beginning of a secular bear market in 2000, described in my previous book *Stock Cycles* now appears to be well established. The forecast of an ordinary bull market to start from the 2002-3 lows made in this book also seems to have come to pass. The remaining stock forecasts are still in the future, and are the reason I am re-issuing the book in a lower-priced paperback edition with wider availability.

On the other hand, the forecast of the "fall from plateau" in reduced prices (see Chapter 4 and Appendix C) has yet to come to pass. Reduced price has continued to move sideways since 2003. As a result we have seen considerably more commodity price inflation that would be expected under the "fall from plateau" scenario. As a result, the gold and oil strategies presented in Chapter 6 have been irrelevant in the past two years and will remain so unless (until) the fall from plateau becomes manifest.

Michael A Alexander
December, 2004

Acknowledgements

I would like to thank Vince Lamb for his detailed editorial input and many helpful suggestions. I would also like to acknowledge the many useful discussions on the Kondratiev cycle and saeculum by participants of the longwaves mail list and Fourth Turning website (www.fourthturning.com), especially Bob Bronson, Bruce Carman, Tom Drake, Bill Tamblyn and Eric von Baranov. Most of all I wish to thank my loving and talented wife Kay for her patience with my writing endeavors.

Chapter 1

Introduction

This book is a continuation of my first book *Stock Cycles*. Writing in early 2000, I forecast that a *secular* (long-term) bear market would probably begin that year. Three years later, it appears I was right. My focus in *Stock Cycles* was to counter the bullish prognostications then popular. I had not given a lot of thought about how one would best invest in a secular bear market. My analysis had suggested that the NASDAQ was already at 1929-like valuations at the 3000 level, and that the idea that it could go much higher was hard to believe. Yet it did.

Amidst this background of incredible stock market advance, I wrote *Stock Cycles* with some trepidation that it might indeed be different this time. It was hard to focus on what to do in a world of NASDAQ 1500 and S&P500 900 when these indices were so much higher than these levels (and heading higher). Today we live in the world I foresaw and the question of what to do about it is paramount on the minds of ordinary investors trying to accumulate enough in their 401K to retire some day. This book attempts to shed some light on what lies in store for this secular bear market.

The key idea in *Stock Cycles* was that stocks move in large-scale secular bull and bear markets. Although over the very long run stocks earn a little under 7% after inflation, the vast majority of this return occurs during the secular bull markets, leaving little for the bear market periods, like now. Because the secular bull market was still in progress at the time *Stock Cycles* was written, the main thrust of the arguments I made was that an investor *should get out of the market* in 2000. Not emphasized was what that investor should do after getting out of the market. The main alternative to stocks implied by the subtitle "why stocks won't beat money markets for the next twenty years" was money markets. In the book I compared projected stock returns with then current ~5% money markets and showed the probability was at least 85% that stocks would fail to beat this return over the next 20 years. I did not discuss the possibility that money markets might also perform abysmally over the next twenty years.

Terrible returns from money-market type investments was a feature of the last deflationary secular bear market in the 1930's and 1940's, but not for previous deflationary secular bear markets. I had thought the Great Depression was an anomaly not to be repeated and so I drew most of my historical analogies about the future from the late 19th century secular bear market and not the 1930's. Since then I have learned more about the economic cycles that affect investment returns and no longer believe that money markets are going to be a viable alternative to stocks. Instead, in order to obtain a modest return, passive long-term investors such as myself will have to manage a portfolio containing different types of stocks and bonds, the mixture of which changes with position in economic cycles.

Long-term, buy-and-hold strategies for bonds and money market funds will also not do very well in this secular bear market. Although bonds are supposed to be the preferred asset class during deflationary secular bear markets like the current one, economic adjustments by the Federal Reserve will tend to reduce the effectiveness of bond investments without greatly improving the situation for stocks. Thus although bonds have performed well in the 2000-2002 bear market and will probably do likewise in the next, they will likely be a terrible investment after that.

A fixed asset allocation can reduce fluctuations in portfolio value, but any mix will only produce the weighted average of the long-term returns of all the asset classes. For example, consider a purchase of a 50:50 mix of bonds and stocks at the beginning of 1931, at which point the stock market had fallen about 50% from its 1929 peak, about as much as the market has fallen from the 2000 peak. Such a mix would have produced a 1-1.5% real return over the remainder of the secular bear market. Mixing in a money market fund would only serve to depress returns still further.

Thus, to obtain a decent return during a secular bear market requires one either develop skills as a stock picker or trader, or practice a dynamic asset allocation strategy. There is no easy solution. For those investors interested in trying their hand at stock picking or trading, there are many excellent books on these topics in bookstores and libraries. For people whose primary retirement portfolio is a 401K account with limited investment options, these strategies are harder to pursue. They are also very difficult skills to master. Some people will desire a more passive strategy that requires few adjustments each year. The general strategy developed in my books is intended for these people. For roughly half of the time, the strategy is extremely simple, employ a 100% stock allocation in an index fund. This half of the time is during secular bull markets like 1982-2000. The whole objective of my first book (written in early 2000) was to argue the case that the 1982-2000 secular bull market was going to end very soon and that a 100% stock allocation was no longer the best place in which to have one's money. The objective for this book is to discuss what strategy a passive 401K investor might consider now that a secular bear market has begun. I will start by sketching out what this secular bear market might look like.

A hypothetical path for the secular bear market

Figure 1.1 shows a hypothetical path for the secular bear market. The purpose of this figure to provide a rough idea of what a secular bear market looks like. In no way should it be construed as a forecast of detailed future market movements. The secular bear market is assumed to end around October 2018 and a new secular bull market begin, which is indicated by the strongly rising line at the extreme right of the figure. There is virtually no chance that the actual path taken by the market during this secular bear market will look exactly like this. The point of this exercise is to show that a secular bear market should not be thought of as a long-term decline to some final bottom. A better way to look at it is as a period during which the stock market is range bound, rather than upward-trending as it is during a secular bull market. Although a long-term buy-and-hold strategy will do poorly, it is possible to do reasonably well in stocks during a secular bear market. It is necessary to practice some sort of timing to do this. The timing could be buying an index at low prices during bear markets and selling at high prices during bull markets, or it could be buying individual stocks or types of stocks when the price is right. The index stock strategy would be coupled with a bond index fund strategy. When stock index fund allocations are rising during the later stages of bear markets, bond index fund allocations are falling. During the later stages of bull markets, allocation would move from stocks to bonds.

To do this one requires some idea of when it is late in a bull or bear market. That is, one requires some information on what the path of the market will be over the next several years in order to make these decisions. Although the path shown in Figure 1.1 is not going to be the actual path taken by the market over the remainder of the secular bear market, there are some features shown that are likely to be approximately true. For example, the figure implies that the secular bear market will end in 2018. Although such an exact date cannot be predicted, it is true that 18 years is the most likely length for this secular bear market if historical parallels hold. Since use of historical parallels *in Stock Cycles* correctly predicted the start of the secular bear market in advance there seems a reasonable chance that similar analysis might reveal other features about this secular bear market. In any case, I will proceed with the assumption that historical analogies still hold.

Figure 1.1. A hypothetical course for the current secular bear market

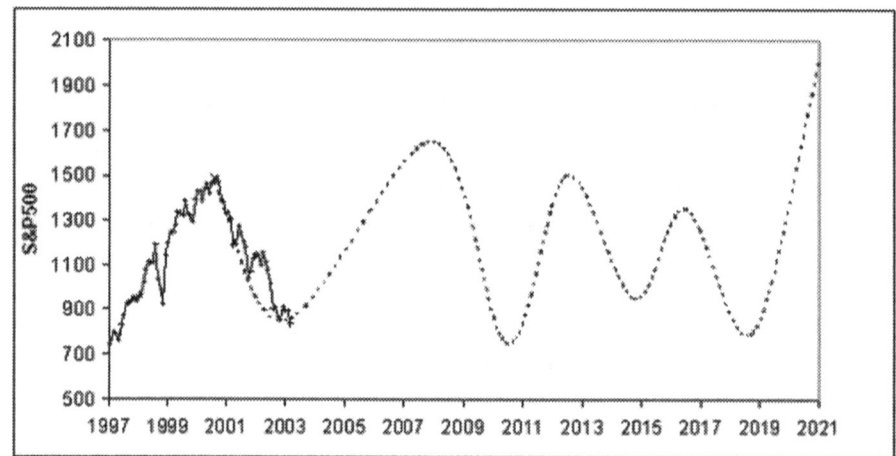

Figure 1.1 also suggests that the current bear market has just about ended and that a new bull market should be beginning. I believe this to be true, as I will describe in the forthcoming chapters. Also suggested is the idea that new highs should be obtained on the S&P500 index before the end of this decade and that this high will be followed by a bear market even greater than the one we have just experienced. Reasons for this belief will also be discussed in the next few chapters. Also shown is the idea that there will be four bull/bear market periods in this secular bear market. Four is just an average, history suggests as few as three or as many as five. The timing for these bull and bear markets in the figure is also not arbitrary. It reflects a shorter historical cycle of some interest that will be described in the next chapter. Nevertheless, one should not assume that the actual future path of the market will look like Figure 1.1; it will not. Rather, the future path and Figure 1.1 will share features in common.

My view of secular bear markets is different from other commentators who view them as simply very long, but still ordinary, bear markets. I believe secular market trends make up a long cycle in the stock market that I call the Stock Cycle. Within this cycle are shorter cycles that comprise ordinary bull and bear markets. Just as a skilled trader can exploit the rallies and corrections during an ordinary bull or bear market, so can a trader exploit the ordinary bull and bear markets during a secular bull or bear market. My view is it is usually not worthwhile to trade the ordinary bull and bear markets during a secular bull market since the general trend over the entire period is sufficiently strong for one to get an excellent return simply through a passive buy-and-hold strategy.

This is not the case during a secular bear market and trading these cycles is a strategy that needs to be seriously considered.

If a secular bear market was the inverse of a secular bull market, that is, a lengthy period during which stocks move downward, then attempting to trade the ordinary bull and bear markets would not be recommended, just as it is not during a secular bull market. But the Stock Cycle is <u>not</u> a cycle in stock *prices*, but rather in stock *valuation*. The "fundamental" that ultimately determines the level of the market (i.e. a broad-based index) is economic growth, which proceeds upward over the long run. In the long run stocks go up.

How fast stocks move up in the shorter run depends on how investors collectively value the current fundamentals. The key idea of the Stock Cycle is that the "market mind" has a cyclical opinion of stock valuations. For long periods of roughly 18 years, it generally becomes ever more optimistic on what stocks should be worth and thus assigns ever higher valuations to stocks based on the steadily rising fundamentals. The result is a secular bull market. Following the secular bull market comes another period, also about 18 years long, during which the market mind becomes increasingly pessimistic on what stocks should be worth and which assigns ever-lower valuations on the same steadily rising fundamentals. The falling valuations counteract the rising fundamentals to produce an 18-year period during which the long-term rising trend in stock prices is temporarily suspended. That is, while stocks show a long-term rising trend during a secular bull market they show a long-term *flat* (not falling) trend during secular bear markets.

There is no overriding trend that a trader must overcome in the secular bear market as there is for the secular bull market. Thus, it should be easier to outperform money markets by trading the bull and bear market cycles during a secular bear market than it is to outperform the stock index during a secular bull market. This book will present what I have learned from additional historical studies intended to provide insight into how this secular bear market may unfold. A few investment strategies are also presented that take advantage of some of the things presented. I also present what I have actually done in my own 401K to show the difficulty of trying to invest during a secular bear market. There can be no guarantee that any of the strategies will work, but I believe that the information presented will permit one to make better investment choices over the next 15 years than one might have otherwise done.

The Stock Cycle and the Kondratiev cycle

Before proceeding, a recap of the findings in my two previous books is in order. *Stock Cycles* introduced the concept of secular market trends: lengthy periods in which stock returns were unusually good or bad. The Stock Cycle was tied to a larger economic cycle called the Kondratiev cycle. Two Stock Cycles made up one Kondratiev cycle. The Kondratiev cycle (or K-cycle for short) is most commonly described as a cycle of monetary factors such as debt, interest rates, and price inflation. It is also often related to a cycle of innovation in which startlingly new economic activities called *basic innovations* appear once per cycle. So pervasive are the changes produced by these basic innovations that they can be said to create a whole new economy. Thus, the K-cycle can also be represented as a series of "innovation waves" that pass through the economy once per cycle, creating a new economy. One sort of basic innovation comes from technological developments leading to new products and industries. For example, the development of the automobile and electric power transformed the economy of Western nations in the early 20th century, creating what I call the mass-production economy. This economy followed an earlier "railroad-industrial economy" which was launched by the development of railroads and new industrial technologies such as low-cost steel making.

New technologies are not the only source of basic innovations. Development of new trade routes, new markets or new business strategies can serve as innovations too. For example, the discovery of the New World and the route to the Indies in the late 15th century transformed the economies of Spain and Portugal, leading to the national greatness of the Iberian nations in the 16th century.

I explored the Kondratiev cycle further in my second book of the same name. I traced the K-cycle using monetary data (mostly prices) back to the 12th century. I also characterized the K-cycle in terms of the innovation wave back to the 14th century. The two cycles corresponded closely enough to support my contention that they were both descriptors of the same underlying economic process. I then showed that the economic K-cycle was itself closely aligned with a social cycle that could be characterized in terms of the level of social unrest. I proposed several models to explain why these two phenomena should be aligned. I then related these aligned social and economic cycles to yet another cycle; the generational cycle called the saeculum. This correspondence introduced the idea of generations as the key timing element controlling the K-cycle and the Stock Cycle. Before exploring the concept of generationally-related economic cycles, a review of the idea of generational cycles is required.

The generational cycle called the saeculum

William Strauss and Neil Howe wrote a fascinating book called *Generations: the History of American's Future* that interprets U.S. history in terms of a repeating series of four basic types of generations. Each generation leaves its own stamp on events of the day, and in turn is shaped by the times. That is, generations shape history and history shapes generations. In their follow up work, *The Fourth Turning*, Strauss and Howe propose that history moves in long cycles, each four generations long, which they call the *saeculum*, after the ancient Etruscan cycle of similar length. Examples of how generations affect one's world view (and actions taken) abound. Thirty years ago it was assumed that people tended to be politically liberal when young and gradually grow more conservative as they age. This idea explained the facts at that time of liberal youth and conservative elders. Yet by the 1990's the situation had reversed, elders tended to be more liberal than young people. The 1980's sitcom *Family Ties* humorously underlined this developing trend with the young arch-conservative Alex Keaton and his liberal parents.

Today's young adults, what is called Generation X, have a collective outlook on life that is more conservative than Baby Boomers had at the same age. This conservative outlook is part of what Strauss and Howe call the *peer personality* of a generation. Generations with similar peer personalities will share beliefs and behavior patterns. For example, the Lost generation, born at the end of the nineteenth century, and Generation X have similar peer personalities, making both of them the same type of generation.

The peer personality of a particular generation is shaped by the generation's historical location relative to a *social moment*. A social moment is an era, typically lasting about a decade, when people perceive that historical events are radically altering their social environment. Thus, a generation's peer personality (what makes it a particular kind of generation) depends on when they were born relative to particularly eventful periods in history. There are two types of social moments: *Secular Crises*, when society focuses on reordering the outer world of institutions and public behavior; and *Spiritual Awakenings*, when society focuses on changing the inner world of values and private behavior.

Table 1.1 lists Secular Crises and Spiritual Awakenings spanning the last 500 years. The last three Secular Crises are easily recognized as momentous times in American history. The social moments in Table 1.1 are spaced about 88 years apart on average. The Secular Crises are located approximately halfway between the Spiritual Awakenings and vice versa. This recurring pattern of alternating Crises and Awakenings define an 88 year cycle which Strauss and Howe maintain reflects a repeating succession of four generations of 22 year length.

Table 1.1. Social moments in American history (from *Generations* p 87)

Cycle	Spiritual Awakening	Secular Crisis
Pre-Colonial	Reformation (1517-1539)	Spanish Armada (1580-1588)
Colonial	Puritan Awakening (1621-1640)	Glorious Revolution (1675-1692)
Revolutionary	Great Awakening (1734-1743)	American Revolution (1773-1789)
Civil War	Transcendental Awakening (1822-1837)	Civil War (1857-1865)
Great Power	Missionary Awakening (1886-1903)	Depression & WWII (1932-1945)
Millennial	Boom Awakening (1967-1980)	--

The four generation and peer personality types are described below (*Generations* p 74)

A dominant, inner-fixated *Prophet* generation grows up as increasingly indulged youths after a Secular Crisis; comes of age inspiring a Spiritual Awakening; fragments into narcissistic rising adults; cultivates principles as moralistic mid-lifers; and emerges as visionary elders guiding the next Secular Crisis. Prophets reflect the *idealist* peer personality. Most recent example is the Boom generation (b 1943-60).

A recessive *Nomad* generation grows up as underprotected and criticized youths during a Spiritual Awakening; matures into risk-taking, alienated rising adults; mellows into pragmatic midlife leaders during a Secular Crisis; and maintains respect (but less influence) as reclusive elders. Nomads reflect the *reactive* peer personality. Most recent example is Generation X (b 1961-81).

A dominant, outer-fixated *Hero* generation grows up as increasingly pro-tected youths after a Spiritual Awakening, comes of age overcoming a Secular Crisis, unites into a heroic and achieving cadre of rising adults, sustains that image while building institutions as powerful midlifers, and emerges as busy elders attacked by the next Spiritual Awakening. Heroes reflect the *civic* peer personality. Most recent example is the GI generation (b 1901-24).

A recessive *Artist* generation grows up as overprotected and suffocated youths during a Secular Crisis; matures into risk-adverse, conformist rising adults; produces indecisive mid-life arbitrator-leaders during a Spiritual Awakening; and maintains influence (but less respect) as sensitive elders. Artists reflect the *adaptive* peer personality. Most recent example is the Silent generation (b 1925-42).

In *The Fourth Turning* (1997) Strauss and Howe develop the concept of *turnings*, historical periods (associated with generations) that show common characteristics just as do generations. Two of these turnings contain the social moments and take their names from them. Hence, an Awakening turning contains the Spiritual Awakening social moment. It is the time when prophets come of age, "a passionate era of spiritual upheaval, when the civic order comes under attack from a new values regime" (Strauss and Howe, 1997b). Similarly, a Crisis turning contains the Secular Crisis social moment. It is the time when Heroes come of age, "a decisive era of secular upheaval, when the values regime propels the replacement of the old civic order with a new one" (Strauss and Howe 1997b).

Stauss and Howe introduce two turnings in-between the social moments. The Unraveling turning, sandwiched between the Awakening and the Crisis, is a "downcast era of strengthening individualism and weakening institutions, when the old civil order decays and a new values regime implants." (Strauss and Howe, 1997b). It is the time when Nomads come of age. Finally, the High turning, located between the Crisis and Awakening, is "an upbeat era of strengthening institutions and weakening individualism, when a new civic order implants and the old values regime decays". This is the time when Artists come of age.

Table 1.2 shows the 25 turnings since 1435 and the 24 generations associated with them. The regular succession of turnings implies a form of cyclical history based on a recurring pattern of four generational types, which Strauss and Howe term the saeculum. Note that the Hero generation that should have come of age during the Civil War Crisis is missing, a phenomenon Strauss and Howe refer to as the Civil War anomaly. This anomaly strongly affects the applicability of their cycle for predictions as shall soon be shown.

In *Generations*, Strauss and Howe characterized generation length as a *phase of life* equal in length to the span between birth and coming of age. Using 22 years as the typical generation length (as suggested by the average spacing of social moments) they identified four phases of life: elders (age 66-87); midlife adults (age 44-65); rising adults (age 22-43); and youth (age 0-21). Each phase-of-life has a central role: *stewardship* for elders, *leadership* for midlife adults, *activity* for rising adults and *dependence* for youth.

One of the key ideas behind their generational approach to history is that "history shapes generations". That is, generations have peer personalities that are shaped by living though a momentous period of history, the social moment. How peer personalities are shaped depends on what phase of life the generation occupies. For example, during a great war, rising adults will do most of the fighting as part of their *active* central role and will develop a heroic character as a result. Elders, as the *stewards* of the values of the society, will produce the moral framework through which the war is viewed as they carry out this role. Mid-life adults, in their *leadership* role, develop the tough character necessary to make the hard decisions of who lives and who dies. Finally, youth stay out of the way in accordance with their *dependent* role.

In the special case when the elders have the Idealist peer personality, the war will be framed as a moral crusade, making the war not just an ordinary crisis, but part of a Secular Crisis turning. The Reactive generation that follows the Idealists will be particularly well-suited to managing the conflict and will ensure that their conservative values will prevail after the war, that is, that a High turning follows the war. The rising adults who fight the war develop the can-do, teamwork characteristics of a Civic generation. It is this generation which will build the comfortable, but stale, culture during the subsequent High. And it is this generation that defends their creation against youthful Idealists during the Awakening that follows.

Table 1.2. List of historical turnings and generations according to Strauss and Howe

Turning (dates)[1]	Turning Type	Associated Generation (birth years)	Generation Type
Retreat from France (1435-1459)	*Unraveling*	*Arthurian (1433-1459)*	*Hero*
War of the Roses (1459-1487)	*Crisis*	*Humanist (1460-1482)*	*Artist*
Tudor Renaissance (1487-1517)	*High*	*Reformation (1483-1511)*	*Prophet*
Protestant Reformation (1517-1542)	*Awakening*	*Reprisal (1512-1540)*	*Nomad*
Intolerance & Martyrdom (1542-1569)	*Unraveling*	*Elizabethan (1541-1565)*	*Hero*
Armada Crisis (1569-1594)	*Crisis*	*Parliamentary (1566-1587)*	*Artist*
Merrie England (1594-1621)	*High*	*Puritan (1588-1617)*	Prophet
Puritan Awakening (1621-1649)	Awakening	Cavalier (1618-1647)	Nomad
Reaction & Restoration (1649-1675)	Unraveling	Glorious (1648-1673)	Hero
Glorious Revolution (1675-1704)	Crisis	Enlightenment (1674-1700)	Artist
Augustan Age of Empire (1704-1727)	High	Awakening (1701-1723)	Prophet
Great Awakening (1727-1746)	Awakening	Liberty (1724-1741)	Nomad
French & Indian Wars (1746-1773)	Unraveling	Republican (1742-1766)	Hero
American Revolution (1773-1794)	Crisis	Compromise (1767-1791)	Artist
Era of Good Feelings (1794-1822)	High	Transcendental (1792-1821)	Prophet
Transcendental Awakening (1822-1844)	Awakening	Gilded (1822-1842)	Nomad
Mexican War & Sectionalism (1844-1860)	Unraveling	*Generation skipped*	Hero
Civil War (1860-1865)	Crisis	Progressive (1843-1859)	Artist
Reconstruction & Gilded Age (1865-1886)	High	Missionary (1860-1882)	Prophet
Third Great Awakening (1886-1908)	Awakening	Lost (1883-1900)	Nomad
World War I & Prohibition (1908-1929)	Unraveling	GI (1901-1924)	Hero
Depression & World War II (1929-1946)	Crisis	Silent (1925-1942)	Artist
American High (1946-1964)	High	Boom (1943-1960)	Prophet
Consciousness Revolution (1964-1984)	Awakening	Generation X (1961-1981)	Nomad
Culture Wars (1984-)	Unraveling	Millennial (1982-?)	Hero

[1]   Entries in italics were presented later in *The Fourth Turning*, not in the initial work *Generations*.

The central role acquired by each generation during the social moment is retained into the next phase of life. That is, long after the war, the war heroes carry their *civic* peer personality traits into mid-life. The tough, midlife war leaders become conservative, *reactionary* elders. Finally the repressed youths mature into compliant *adaptive* rising adults, content to let the older heroes continue to call the shots during the postwar High.

Another key idea of their model is carryover can continue for one generation (or turning), but not two. That is, after two phases of life pass, roles must be reassigned. In my war example, a new *Prophet* generation in rising adulthood, having had no experience with the war and unwilling to defer to the Heroes of that war, demand a re-ordering of the Hero-created world. Adaptive next-elders then must take on leadership roles, serving as brokers between their heroic next-elder and fiery next-younger generations. This period, of course, is the Awakening turning. With the no-nonsense Nomads gone, the less tough Heroes and pliable Artist generations cannot deal with their boisterous juniors and social change results. Rising adult Prophets develop the self-assured idealist peer personality where they *know* what is right and should be done, unlike their dithering Artist next elders or their out-of-touch Hero parents. The next generation of Nomads grows up in the moral flux of the Awakening without a clear set of values and develops a pragmatic, experiential view of life. They make the most of the opportunities presented during the highly individualistic Unraveling, and then, as they age, produce a stable, centered society that is the opposite of the fragmented world they inherited.

The moral certainty produced by the Awakening in the Prophet generation is what allows them to frame the crisis that occurs later in their life in terms of a moral crusade—what makes it a Secular Crisis. The pragmatic, reactive peer-personality of Nomads, forged during the Awakening, is what gives them the conservative world-view that produces the High after the Crisis. The civic peer personality of the Hero generation, forged in the fire of the Crisis, creates the well-ordered world targeted during the Awakening turning. Similarly, the equivocal, balanced adaptive peer personality of the Artist archetype, produced by a childhood during a Crisis, permits the individuality and cultural experimentation of the Unraveling. This is the central idea: the interaction of a particular generational constellation generates social moments (generations shape history) which themselves influence generations (history shapes generations).

Strauss and Howe introduce two more assumptions that strengthen the four-stroke cycle. (1) During each social moment, each generation will redefine the central role of the phase of life it is entering in a direction that reverses the perceived excesses of that role since the last social moment. (2) Each generation has a formative nurturing relationship primarily with the other two-apart generation, in which they try to cultivate a peer-personality they perceive as complimentary to their own. For example, Prophets, perceiving the role of the Heroes as too stultifying, rebel against their communitarian, team-playing ethic during an Awakening. Yet later in life, they raise their children to be Heroes. Similarly, Heroes rebel against a world of individualism where institutions do not work, accomplish great things through teamwork during a Secular Crisis and build new institutions during a High. Yet they raise their own children to be Prophets. This process results in adjacent social moments having a very different character from each other, giving rise to the alternating pattern of Spiritual Awakenings and Secular Crises. The result is the four-stroke cycle that Strauss and Howe call the saeculum.

Central to this mechanism of generational change is the idea that generations reflect a phase of life, which is about 22 years long. The mechanism won't function if the generational length is much longer or shorter than this 22 year length. With 30 year generations, for example, elderhood begins at age 90. It is apparent that no significant role can be played by nonagenarian elders. Similarly it is hard to imagine much of a nurturing relationship between generations spaced two 30-year generations apart. Similarly, 15 year generations would have elderhood beginning at age 45, with people over 60 too old to play any role in the cycle at all.

A relatively fixed generation length is a prerequisite for using the generational cycle to make predictions. We entered an Unraveling turning in 1984 (see Table 1.2). At some point this turning will end and a new one, a Crisis turning, will begin. Using the average generational length of 22 years, Strauss and Howe predict a "crisis of 2020":

> *When will the crisis come?* The climatic event may not arrive exactly in the year 2020, but it won't arrive much sooner or later. A cycle is the length of four generations, or roughly eighty-eight years. If we plot a half-cycle ahead from the Boom Awakening (and find the forty-fourth anniversaries of Woodstock and the Reagan Revolution), we project a crisis lasting from 2013 to 2024. If we plot a full cycle ahead from the last secular crisis (and find the eighty-eighth anniversaries of the FDR landslide and Pearl Harbor Day), we project a crisis lasting from 2020-2029. By either measure, the early 2020's appear fateful (Generations, p 381)

This excerpt shows an application of a fixed cycle length to predict the start of the next Crisis turning sometime in the second decade of the 21st century.

Events following the terrorist attack on September 11, 2001 in some respects resemble what one might expect of a Crisis turning, although it is really too early to tell. If it is later determined that a crisis turning did indeed begin in 2001, the prediction made in *Generations* (based on an assumption of a fixed 22 year generation/turning length) will have been more than a decade late.

The three most recent generations aren't really very consistent with a 22 year average length. Not only that, but the spacing between the election of FDR and the "Summer of Love" or WW II and the first term of Ronald Reagan, was about 35-40 years, suggesting a 19-20 year generational length rather than 22 years. Indeed of the eight generations since the skipped Civil War Hero generation, only two were longer than 22 years. Their average length, at just under 20 years, suggests that the true length of recent generations might not be a full 22 years. This 20-year average length reflects the fact that the eight most recent generations are assigned to a period that should contain nine generations. Without the Civil War anomaly, the average length of generations would be even shorter. This is shown by the average length of 18 years for the nine most recent turnings.

All these observations suggest that generational length since the Civil War anomaly has been significantly less that the 22-year typical length suggested by Strauss and Howe's phase-of-life model. The ten generations before the anomaly average 25.5 years in length, significantly longer than the 22-year average length. This observation implies that generational length has fallen over time, rather than remain constant at about 22 years. Nevertheless, average lengths of 20-25 years are not completely inconsistent with the phase of life interpretation of generations made in Generations.

Compelling evidence against the interpretation of a generation as a phase of life emerged with Strauss and Howe's subsequent book, *The Fourth Turning*. This book introduced six additions to the list of historical generations (see entries in italics in Table 1.2). These six new generations averaged 26 years in length and when combined with the four colonial generations, showed a group of ten contiguous generations, whose average length of 27 years is simply inconsistent with a phase of life. In *The Fourth Turning*, Strauss and Howe acknowledge that generation length has been trending downward over the centuries. They give 2005 as their prediction for the beginning of the next Secular Crisis turning, only 76 years after the beginning of the last one. This tacit acknowledgement that generations may be as short as 19 years today, while once they were almost 50% longer provides the final evidence to conclude that generation length does not reflect a phase of life.

Relation of the saeculum to economic cycles

In *The Kondratiev Cycle*, I proposed an alternate explanation for generational length that explains their 26-27 year length in the 15th through 17th centuries and their 23-24 year length during the 18th century. From Medieval times to the late 17th century social moment turnings were aligned with Kondratiev upwaves, that is, times of rising prices. I hypothesized that alternating period of rising and falling prices (the K-cycle) were caused of alternating periods of greater and lesser population pressure on the food supply, caused by a lagged effect of population growth on food availability. During good times people would tend to marry earlier and have more children, leading to more adults and greater pressure on food supplies (i.e. bad times) a generation later. The generation experiencing bad times would tend to marry later, reducing their own fertility, which would show up as a relatively smaller population of adults the generation after that. The result of this oscillating fertility would be alternating periods of low population pressure (falling prices, good times) and high population pressure (rising prices, bad times). The bad times are social moments and the good times the turnings in between. These periods (turnings) would be a biological generation (ca. 27 years) in length. Two biological generations would complete one cycle in prices, which is the Kondratiev cycle, which over the long run has averaged 53 years in length. Thus, the saeculum contains two K-cycles.

Kondratiev upwaves, being times of inflation, are good times for debtors. In late Medieval and early modern times, the biggest debtors were monarchs who borrowed funds to make war. By the 17th century, a cycle of warfare had come to be aligned with the Kondratiev cycle. Warfare was substantially more intense during upwaves than downwaves. As nations developed more elaborate means to finance their wars, the fighting of wars, or more properly the accumulation of debt to fight wars, began to have its own effect on prices and interest rates, which reinforced the K-cycle. Upwaves became times of increasing money supply leading to general inflation as well as times of rising food shortages and food prices. Similarly, downwaves were not only times of relative food abundance, but times of general deflation. These financial effects ultimately reversed the relation between the K-cycle and the saeculum. While downwaves were a time of relative food abundance due to lower population pressures, the resulting low food prices did little good for the urban worker left unemployed by the bankruptcy of his employer. Thus, social moment turnings shifted from an upwave to a downwave phenomenon around 1700. This shift in alignment between the K-cycle and the saeculum meant the two saecula between 1675 and 1860 spanned only 3.5 K-cycles instead of four, implying a 13% drop in saeculum length. Such a drop in length is manifested by the shift from ~27 year generations before 1700 to ~23 year generations for more than a century afterward.

I also suggested that there was sufficient room for nine 18-year generations between the Transcendentals and Generation X instead of the eight 20-year generations Strauss and Howe list. This implies a sudden drop in generation length occurred early in the 19th century. It also meant that the Saeculum had become uncoupled from the K-cycle. Only after 1929, did the two cycles re-align, with the K-cycle lengthening from ~53 years to 72 years to encompass four 18-year generations. This means that since 1929, the K-cycle and saeculum have been the same cycle, both reflecting an underlying 18-year generation. I attributed the change in generation length to industrialization, but did not supply any mechanism for how industrialization had produced the change, nor why an 18-year generation length should emerge.

Table 1.3. Alternate generations and turnings 1794-present

Turning	Type	Generation	Type
Era of Good Feelings (1794-1822)	High	Transcendental (1792-1817)	Prophet
Transcendental Awakening (1822-1842)	Awakening	Gilded (1818-1838)	Nomad
Mexican War & Sectionalism (1842-1860)	Unraveling	Civil War Heroes (1839-1856)	Hero
Civil War & Reconstruction (1860-1877)	Crisis	Progressive (1857-1873)	Artist
Gilded Age (1877-1894)	High	Missionary (1874-1890)	Prophet
Third Great Awakening (1894-1912)	Awakening	Lost (1891-1907)	Nomad
World War I & Prohibition (1912-1929)	Unraveling	GI (1908-1924)	Hero
Depression & World War II (1929-1946)	Crisis	Silent (1925-1942)	Artist
American High (1946-1964)	High	Boom (1943-1960)	Prophet
Consciousness Revolution (1964-1982)	Awakening	Generation X (1961-1979)	Nomad
Culture Wars (1982-2001)	Unraveling	Millennial (1980-1998?)	Hero

In the next chapter I present information about shorter economic cycles. One of these cycles is in land values and construction activity. It is associated with periodic financial panics and severe depressions and shows an average length of 18 years. The first panic occurred in 1819, right around the time 18-year generations appeared. Table 1.3 shows a list of alternate turnings for the 1860-1929 period based on this cycle, and the generations that would be associated with it. This scheme introduces a new generation of heroes for the Civil War.

Based on the idea of 18-year generations and alignment of the saeculum with the K-cycle (and by extension the Stock Cycle) I forecasted the beginning of the next Crisis turning with the stock market peak in 2000 (Alexander,

2000b). With the aftermath from the terrorist attack in September 2001, the idea that we entered a Crisis turning in 2001 seems plausible, supporting the thesis that long-term stock movements reflect generational dynamics.

The main purpose for the introduction of generational dynamics is to establish two key concepts. One is that the fundamental unit of measure today in long cycles in finance, economics, politics and social trends is 18 years. The other is my assessment of where in the cycle we currently are located. Determining the correct position within the relevant cycles is an essential requirement in order to use historical analogy to provide insight into what the future may hold. The concepts presented here are contrary to views of many other cycle theorists. This is extremely important. If our current position within the cycles were self-evident, then any predictions made based on this assessment would be necessarily wrong because other market participants, having the same information, would have already acted on it, thus changing the future and rendered the predictions worthless.

Each conclusion I present in this book is one of several that could be reached by considering one or another of the cycles I describe. There is a standard interpretation for each of the cycles I discuss which if employed by itself will lead to a different conclusion than the one I present. For example, in the section above I presented a slightly modified version of the Strauss and Howe saeculum in which we are currently within a secular crisis turning, rather than still within the unraveling turning. This is important, because in a secular crisis, the unorthodox is the norm, and can be expected. Thus, many of unorthodox things that I predict, such as a new bull market starting from record-high valuations, can occur.

The strategy I have taken is to characterize every cycle for which I could find adequate data and then to look for alignment between them. As a result of this work I have concluded that cycles like the Kondratiev or the saeculum are imperfect reflections of an underlying fundamental cyclic socioeconomic process. Using this idea I have modified the various cycles to explicitly reflect this alignment for today. As a result, my version of the K-cycle is a non-standard one (I believe it is 72 years long instead of the standard ~53 year length) as is my saeculum (also 72 years instead of the standard 80-90 years). This allows me to make predictions that differ from those that would be obtained from consideration of only one of the standard cycles.

For example, the financial writer Harry Dent (1998) projected the continuation of the secular bull market to the 2007-2010 period, by which time the Dow would reach 23,000-35,000. Dent based this projection on a demographic argument, which closely agreed with a projection based on an economic version of the saeculum cycle. The combination of the two ideas made a compelling presentation of the case for a continued bull market until close to 2010, after which there would be a another great depression. The appearance of this depression agreed very well with the projected timing for a coming secular crisis made by Strauss and Howe in *Generations*. Dent's economic cycle associated with his demographics was based on the saeculum and shared its timing, namely an 80 year cycle length. The "long boom" concept of the futurist Roger Cass shows an example of the same approach as Dent's, except a different cycle is used. Cass employs a standard Kondratiev cycle to forecast a long boom powered by new internet technology that will last to 2020 or thereabouts (Schwartz and Leyden, 1997).

Dent's economic cycle does an excellent job of explaining economic developments over the past century or so, but it does not work before then. In contrast, the standard Kondratiev cycle does a rather poor job of explaining recent economic events, but works much better for those of the past.

Neither model accounts for the severe bear market that began in 2000. The hybrid model I developed in which the Kondratiev cycle and saeculum are aligned along the lines implied by Dent, but with the 18 year generational timing instead of 20 years does call for the severe bear market at the time it has actually occurred. Curiously, now that a secular bear market has begun, a recent demographic analysis (Geanakoplos et al, 2002) has called for a secular bear market that should last until about 2018, exactly along the lines I forecast based on 18 year generations. If the analysis of Geanakoplos and co-workers is grafted onto my generationally-based K-cycle, one obtains a new version of the Dentian scheme that calls for a secular bear market to begin in 2000 and not 2007.

In the next chapter, I present evidence for a set of shorter cycles that lie within the realm of the Stock Cycle. These cycles will help establish my case for why a new bull market can begin after 2002. In the subsequent chapter, three valuation methods are compared with respect to their accuracy at predicting the top of the bull market and to what they have to say about valuation in 2002. In Chapter Four I present a monetary view of the secular bear market discussing the concept of regime change and its implications for gold and bonds. Next I present how I invested my own 401K during the initial portion of this secular bear market, to give an example of the difficulties posed by a secular bear market. Chapter Six presents some ideas for investment strategies over the next decade or so. Finally Chapter Seven outlines some parameters for the extent of the coming bull market.

Chapter 2

Shorter Business Cycles

In my first book, *Stock Cycles*, I presented evidence that the stock market shows long term bullish and bearish trends that last 7-20 years. I called these trends secular bull and bear markets to distinguish them from ordinary bull and bear markets that typically are much shorter. Adjacent secular bull and bear markets defined the Stock Cycle, which has averaged 28 years in length over the last two centuries. (NB: Stock Cycle is capitalized in this book to distinguish it from the shorter stock cycles defined by ordinary bull and bear markets). I also presented a novel valuation measure that I called price to resources (P/R) which can be used to track the cycle, and to give an indication of when a change in trend was imminent. Based on the unprecedented (high) value of P/R, I concluded that "the current upwards trend in stock index levels will end, most likely this year (2000) but almost certainly by 2004".

I also noted that there were two kinds of Stock Cycle, real and monetary. A real Stock Cycle is caused by changes in the ability of companies to produce earnings. The bull portion of the real cycle reflects strong earnings growth while the bear portion reflects weak earnings growth. A monetary cycle is caused by changes in inflationary characteristics of the economy. The bull portion of a monetary cycle reflects falling inflation while the bear portion is associated with rising inflation. The recently completed Stock Cycle from 1966 to 2000 was of the monetary type, with definite implications for the next cycle (the one which we are in now) as I noted in *Stock Cycles*:

> The situation today (early 2000) is similar to 1929. The effect of both the monetary conditions and a very optimistic assessment of the earnings growth still to come are priced into the index. This is shown by the extraordinarily high level of P/R. I should expect the current monetary cycle to be followed by a real cycle. It should start with a secular bear market in which lower earnings growth will be the problem, not inflation. (Alexander, 2000a).

The idea that there are two kinds of Stock Cycle suggests that there exists an economic cycle that functions on the scale of two Stock Cycles, one real and one monetary. This cycle should be around 56 years long. There is such a cycle,

23

the Kondratiev cycle (K-cycle), which I had learned about only a few months before I wrote *Stock Cycles*. Only after I had become familiar with the Kondratiev cycle, was I convinced that the observations I had made about the stock market were related to an underlying real economic phenomenon. It was only then that I felt confident enough to write a book about the Stock Cycle. By relating my Stock Cycle to another cycle, which has been independently described by many researchers, I believed I had found a mechanistic explanation for *why* the Stock Cycle happened in the first place (and why it should continue to happen in the future). It was simply the natural consequence of the K-cycle.

A troubling problem was the fact that the majority of economists do not believe that there *is* a K-cycle. I presented a brief overview of the K-cycle and one explanation for how it functions in *Stock Cycles*, but the lack of certainty in the fundamental existence of this central cycle remained a problem with the Stock Cycle hypothesis. I concluded my discussion with the idea that a successful prediction of a secular bear market made in *Stock Cycles* could itself serve as evidence for the existence of the K-cycle:

> In a way, this book represents a test of the longwave (K-cycle) by making a specific prediction that a non-inflationary secular bear market will start between 2000 and 2004 and last at least until 2010, and quite probably, longer. (p 158)

I followed *Stock Cycles* with a second book on the Kondratiev cycle, in which I developed the idea that the K-cycle is fundamentally generational in nature. I presented a detailed account of the progress of the K-cycle over the past 800 years and showed that it closely corresponded with the saeculum, a four-generation cycle described by the American authors William Strauss and Neil Howe(1997). Since the economy became fully industrialized in the early 20th century the relation between the cycles changed. Instead of two K-cycles per saeculum, as was the case for hundreds of years before industrialization, there was now only one. As a result, the K-cycle lengthened and the saeculum shortened to the point where both are about 72 years long today. This new pattern has only become fully developed after 1929.

Each Kondratiev cycle consists of two Kondratiev waves, each associated with a Stock Cycle. The Kondratiev upwave is an inflationary period when interest rates show a rising trend. The downwave is deflationary with falling interest rates. The Kondratiev wave is subdivided into two Kondratiev seasons, each associated with a secular market trend. The portion of the upwave associated with a secular bull market is Kondratiev spring. The upwave secular bear market is Kondratiev summer. Similarly, the downwave secular bull market is Kondratiev fall and the secular bear market is Kondratiev winter. The upwave and downwave Stock Cycles are *not* the same as the real and monetary cycles. The real Stock Cycle is composed of Kondratiev winter and spring, while the monetary cycle consists of Kondratiev summer and fall. We entered Kondratiev winter with the stock peak in 2000.

Table 2.1. Structure of socioeconomic cycle periods

Cycle	Pre-industrial (before 1860)	Modern (after 1929)
Saeculum	Two K-cycles (90-115 years)	One K-cycle (72 years)
K-cycle	45-60 years	72 years
K-wave/Stock Cycle	Biological gen (20-30 years)	36 years
K-season/Secular Trend	10-15 years	18-year generation/turning

Prior to industrialization, Kondratiev waves were about 26-27 years on average, roughly equal to generations of biological length, and were associated with turnings, the name Strauss and Howe give to 1/4 of a saeculum. After industrialization, Kondratiev seasons, not waves, have been associated with turnings. Table 2.1 shows how these cycles were related before and after industrialization. In this chapter I will identify the shorter economic/financial cycles, noting how they were affected by industrialization. In particular, I will focus on evidence for a generational influence on the shorter cycles.

Business cycles and primary trends in the stock market

In *Stock Cycles* I described how the Kondratiev seasons could be identified as positive and negative deviations in GDP from its long-term trend. In that analysis, a running 100-year trend in GDP was calculated and the ratio of GDP to this trend plotted. The result was a graph which showed a number of short-term fluctuations lasting a few years and longer term waves which defined the Kondratiev seasons. In Appendix A, I use this same type of analysis to obtain approximate dates for historical short-term business cycles from 1789 onward. The cycles so identified were compared to the list of business cycles since 1854 produced by the National Bureau of Economic Research (NBER). A reasonably good correspondence was obtained for the post 1854 cycles, suggesting that the pre-1854 cycles I obtained using the GDP deviation method are sufficiently accurate for the broad sort of analysis I wish to use in this chapter. The complete list of business expansions and recessions appears in Table A.2 in Appendix A.

Besides the evidence for shorter economic cycles provided by the NBER business cycles and GDP fluctuations before 1854, there is the historical record of trends in stock prices. The study of market fluctuations, with the aim of predicting future market behavior, is called technical analysis. Charles Dow (1851-1902) was the first to categorize stock fluctuations and for this he is sometimes called the "father of technical analysis". He identified three time scales of market action: primary, secondary and minor (Arnold, 1993). Primary trends are broad movements that usually last 4-6 years. A rising primary trend is called a *bull market* and a falling trend a *bear market*. The major advance in the market that started in October 1998 and ended in March 2000 is an example of a bull market. The major decline that began afterward is a bear market. Secondary trends are the corrections and rallies during bull markets or the declines and counter rallies during bear markets. Normally, they last a few weeks to several months. The rally from September 2001 to March 2002 is an example of a secondary trend. The minor trends are short-term movements that usually last less than a week.

The combination of a bull market and a bear market defines a stock cycle that I will call the bull/bear cycle. Several of these bull/bear cycles fall into one Stock Cycle. In Dow's day, bull/bear cycles correlated well with business cycles, but with a six month lead. There was no government-provided economic data in those days and so the behavior of the stock market provided the only real-time assessment of economic conditions. Dow developed the indices that bear his name in order to track this behavior. As a further measure of shorter economic cycles, I assembled a list of bear market primary trends in Table B.1 in Appendix B. The troughs of these bear markets can be used to define the bull/bear cycle. Selecting bear markets (or bull markets) is not as straightforward as it sounds. I use a method proposed by the market researcher Robert Bronson (2002) to measure the "severity" of a market decline, which can then serve as part of the definition of a bear market. Bear market severity, as defined by Bronson, can be approximated by the product of the size of the fluctuation and its length:

Eq. 2.1. severity = log (peak value/bottom value) x length of decline in months

This measure puts more emphasis on long, slow declines than on short, sharp ones. Using this measure of severity and several other considerations, a definition for bear market was developed and used to find all bear markets since 1802. The procedure is described in Appendix B.

The first thing to look at is how the spacing of bear markets and economic recessions have changed over time. Figure 2.1 shows the spacing of bear markets (which defines a bull/bear market cycle) and that of recessions (which defines the business cycle) from the end of the 18th century to the present. Several features are immediately apparent from this figure. The first is that the stock market and the economy showed cycles of similar length up until around 1930, after which the economic cycles have averaged longer than the stock cycles. This says that until 1930, bull/bear cycles could serve as a second measure of the business cycle, providing some confidence that the conclusions drawn about business cycles prior to 1854 are valid. Thus, one can use the term business cycle to refer to either type of cycle.

Figure 2.1. Business cycle length and bear market spacing over time

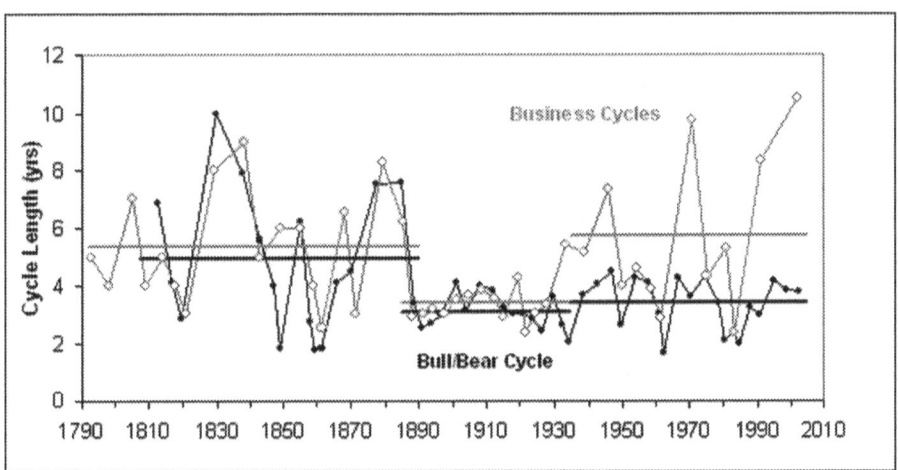

The second feature is that prior to 1885 business cycles were longer (about 5-6 years on average) than during the 1885-1930 period, when they averaged 41 months. The 1885-1930 business cycle length is similar to that of the 40-month inventory liquidation cycle first identified by Joseph Kitchin (1923). This shift in average cycle length in the 1880's is coincident with the time when agriculture ceased to be the dominant economic activity in the US. The Kitchin cycle reflects fluctuations in inventories of (manufactured) consumer durable goods (Furfero, 2000). It can be thought of a cycle in the non-agricultural (manufacturing) economy. It would not be expected to strongly affect the business cycle for the entire economy as long as agriculture remained its dominant element. Only when agriculture shrank to less than half the economy in the 1880's might Kitchin cycles be expected to determine the cycle of overall economic activity. This idea implies that the pre-1885 business cycle operated on some cycle other than the Kitchin.

The third feature is that the bull/bear cycle, which shortened along with the business cycle in the 1880's, remained at this shorter length until the present. That is, it did not rise again in length in recent decades as the business cycle has. These shifts in business and bull/bear cycle lengths define three eras of interest: the pre-industrial (before 1885) the industrial (1885-1933) and the regulated (after 1933).

The Juglar cycle

One of the salient features of U.S. financial history in the 19th and early 20th centuries was the fairly regular occurrence of financial panics at roughly 18 year intervals: 1819, 1837, 1857, 1873, 1893, 1907 and 1929 (Hoyt, 1970). One can use the major bear-market bottoms associated with these panics to define a "panic cycle". Figure 2.2 shows a plot of the stock index from 1815 to 1935 in which major stock bottoms are identified. Seven of these bottoms (in bold) were the ultimate low of a decline beginning with one of these panics (in italic bold). Hence, panics in 1819, 1837, 1857, 1873, 1893, and 1907 produced declines that bottomed in 1819, 1842, 1857, 1877, and 1907, respectively. The stock market crash in 1929 began a decline that ended in 1932.

Figure 2.2. Financial panics and the Kuznets and Juglar cycles defined by them

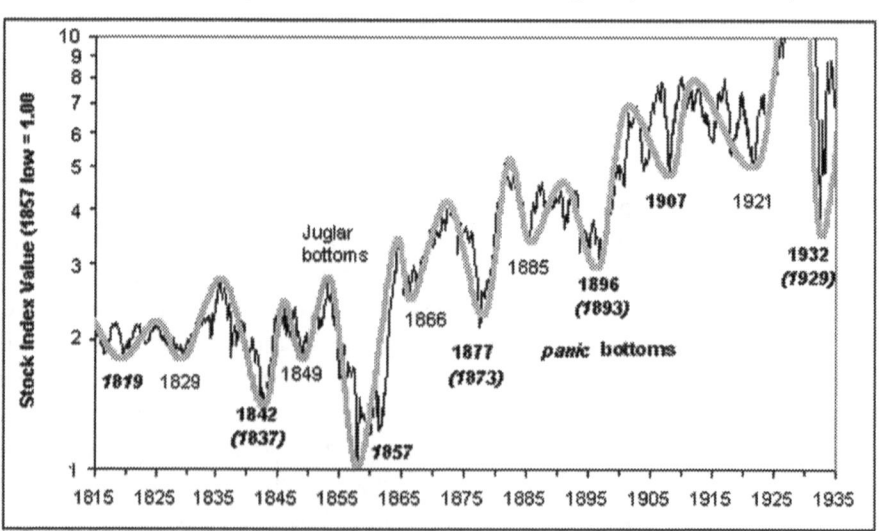

In between these panic bottoms there are other major lows that are also identified in Figure 2.2 in plain type. The combination of both of these troughs defines a shorter 7-14 year cycle (average 10 years) that is (usually) half of a panic cycle. This cycle is outlined by the heavy gray line in Figure 2.2. The first description of shorter business cycles was made by Clement Juglar in 1862. Juglar noted a cycle of 7-11 years that he related to fluctuations in fixed investments. The half-panic cycle described above has the same length as the cycles described by Juglar and so I will denote them as Juglar cycles.

Since the Depression there have been no financial panics so the method used to find Juglar cycles in Figure 2.2 cannot be applied. The 12 regular business cycles since 1933 average 68 months in length, much longer than the 41 month average during the 1885-1933 period (Figure 2.1). The standard deviation of the post-1933 business cycle lengths is very large (47% of average length) compared to that for the industrial period (22% of average length). This degree of dispersion is even greater than what one would expect for cycles of random length. Closer examination shows that they appear to fall into two categories: eight short cycles of 28 to 64 months in length (average 49) and four long cycles of 88 to 125 months in length (average 108). A t-test (a measure of statistical significance) on these two sets of cycles shows the hypothesis that there exist two populations of modern business cycles with two lengths is significant at only the 80% level (95% is usually considered significant). If the closely-spaced recessions in 1980 and 1982 are considered as a single "double-dip" recession, there would be 11 business cycles since 1933 that fall into two categories, long cycles of 105±16 months and short cycles of 50±9 months. These two populations are statistically different at the >96% confidence level.

These two classes of cycles have rather small standard deviations relative to length (15% and 18%), similar to the tight dispersion of the industrial cycles. This suggests that each cycle has its own mechanism, just like industrial era business cycles were linked to inventory (Kitchin) cycles. The shorter cycle is close to the length of the pre-1933 business cycle, which I have already ascribed to the action of the Kitchin cycle. It is also roughly equivalent to the length of the bull/bear cycles after 1933. Thus I characterize both the shorter business cycle and the bull/bear cycle in the post-1933 period as Kitchin cycles. The longer 9 year business cycle is then considered to reflect a Juglar cycle.

The Kuznets cycle

The "panic cycle" in Figure 2.2 corresponds reasonably well to the pre-depression U.S. real estate cycle. Land sales by the US government before the

Civil War showed massive peaks in activity in 1818, 1836 and 1854 followed by sharp drops to troughs in 1820, 1841 and 1860 (Hoyt, 1970). Chicago land values showed similar peaks in 1836, 1854, 1872, 1891, and 1925 and troughs in 1840, 1859, 1875, 1894 and 1933 (Hoyt, 1970). The number of new buildings constructed in Chicago showed major peaks in 1892, 1910 and 1925 and troughs in 1900, 1918 and 1933.

Figure 2.3. Building Activity* 1885 to present

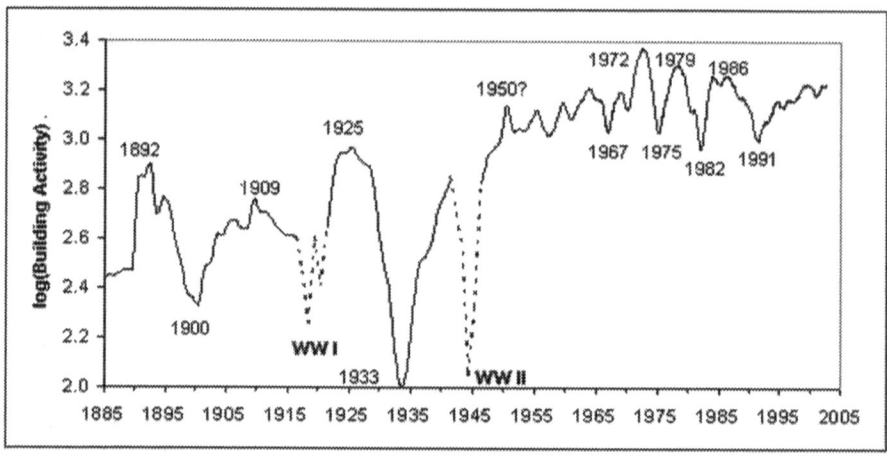

* Housing starts after 1960 (from economagic.com). New non-farm dwelling units for 1900-1960, and building construction in Chicago before 1900 (Data from Hoyt, 1970). All values in thousands of units per year. Housing starts and new non-farm dwelling units appear to be the same series. The Chicago series was used to extrapolate the housing start series back from 1900 to 1885.

Combining these observations shows an 18-year cycle in real estate with peaks in 1818, 1836, 1854, 1872, 1891, 1910 and 1925. The first five of these peaks in real estate were closely followed by a financial panic (1819, 1837, 1857, 1873, 1893) suggesting a correspondence between the real estate and the panic cycle during the 19th century. The American economist Simon Kuznets discovered the Kuznets cycle of about 15-20 years in length in 1930, which he related to building construction activity. It would seem the real-estate/panic cycle is a Kuznets cycle.

Although financial panics became a thing of the past after 1933, the Kuznets cycle can continue to be tracked by consideration of fluctuations in the real estate market. Figure 2.3 presents a graph of building activity from 1885 to the present. Peaks in building activity can be seen in 1892, 1909 and 1925, which reflect the pre-depression Kuznets cycle. Ignoring WW II, after the trough in 1933 there was a smoothly rising trend in building activity that reached a peak in 1950. This peak was not followed by a conventional bust, but rather a plateau. It was not until the late 1960's that something like an old-fashioned real estate boom developed. This boom peaked in 1972 and was followed by a bust which bottomed in 1975. This boom/bust cycle was immediately followed by two more which showed peaks in 1979 and 1986, and troughs in 1982 and 1991. Since 1991 building activity has shown a more leisurely rise and has yet to show any sort of peak.

Figure 2.4. Real housing price index (1982=1.0)

Figure 2.4 shows a housing price index obtained by dividing the GDP implicit residential deflator by the total GDP implicit deflator as described by McFadden (1994). This McFadden index reflects the trend in real housing values *without* land included. A series of peaks in 1873, 1887, 1907 and 1929 can be seen which roughly correlate with peaks in Chicago land values in 1872, 1891 and 1925, and with those in building activity in 1892, 1909, and 1925. Thus, Figures 2.3 and 2.4 describe a pre-1933 Kuznets real estate cycle that is consistent with the panic-related Kuznets cycle described earlier. Both figures show a major rise in both housing construction and price after the 1933 cycle bottom that lasted until around 1950. Both show no significant decline in values or activity commensurate with a bust after this date. A boom in housing prices developed only after the 1970 recession and lasted the entire decade. There was no intermediate peak in 1972 as there was for building activity, however. Likewise, there was no peak in the mid-1980's as was seen with building

activity. Both series show troughs in the early 1990's and a rise afterward. If the price peak in 1969 is interpreted as a separate peak, and troughs assigned at the price minima in 1958 and 1971, one can see what appears to be a continuation of the Kuznets cycle after 1933 in Figure 2.4. This pattern is not supported by the building activity data.

Further insight may be gained by examining median housing prices, which are available after 1963 for new houses and after 1970 for existing houses. Figure 2.5 shows a plot of these prices in constant 2002 dollars. Also shown are ratios of the housing price to income, which might be thought of as a type of "valuation" for housing, sort of like P/E for stocks. Income of the 65th percentile of households (the middle of the top 70% of households) was chosen as reflective of the income of the "typical" home buyer, and thus most comparable to the median home price. Prices for existing homes have tended to trend with income; that is, the ratio between price and income is range bound. This ratio defines a cycle with a peak in 1978-9 and trough around 1990, followed by a slow recovery. Since 2000 a steeper uptrend appears to have gotten underway, suggestive of the beginning of another boom. This data is consistent with the McFadden index in Figure 2.4, which suggests only one peak in the 1970-1990 period and not three as suggested by housing starts in Figure 2.3.

Figure 2.5. Median real housing prices and the ratio of price* to household income

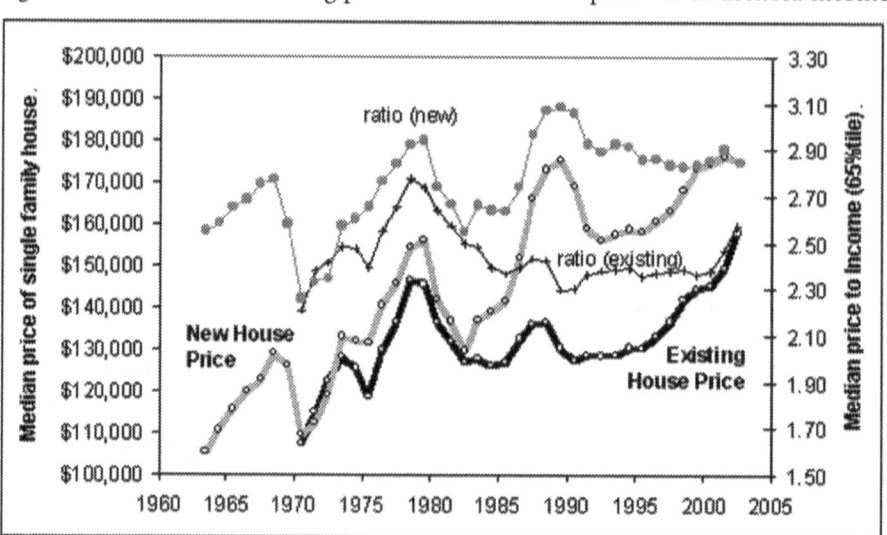

* Prices for new homes were obtained from census data. Data for existing homes after 1989 come from the National Association of Realtors and from the statistical abstract of the US before 1989.

Prices for new homes in constant dollars have shown a consistent rise over time with noticeable peaks in 1969, 1979 and 1989. The ratio between new house prices and income also displays a rising trend over time with three clear peaks corresponding to the price peaks. The first two of these peaks are consistent with McFadden peaks in Figure 2.4, the third is not. The different trends for new versus existing houses after the early 1980's in Figure 2.5 suggests that price behavior of new houses is responding to something that does not apply to existing houses. An obvious difference between new and existing houses over time is that a typical new house can be built bigger and better than the average existing house. That is, part of the rising trend in new house price can reflect increased quality and not price inflation. Rising quality in existing houses over time would be much more muted. The McFadden index can be thought of as a *quality-adjusted* real price index for residential construction (McFadden, 1994). Thus, the correspondence between the existing house price index (which is inherently largely quality-adjusted) and the McFadden index makes sense, even though the latter is based on new housing. The strong possibility that the post-1980 trends in the new housing price/income ratios reflect rising quality and not inherent valuation suggests that the Kuznets cycle described by the existing-house price data and the McFadden index is the correct one.

The evidence from prices suggest that an attenuated real estate cycle continued on after 1933 that grew in strength after 1970. The building activity data since 1933 doesn't show this. The minor fluctuations in building activity between 1950 and 1972 closely follow the ordinary business cycle and not some longer cycle. The fluctuations grow larger after 1970 but they continue to reflect the ordinary business cycle and not a longer cycle like prices do. Thus, it appears that building activity no longer follows a Kuznets real estate cycle in the post-1933 era, whereas prices still do.

A real estate sell off in 1798 (Gaffney, 1990) provides another Kuznets trough. With this I can construct a complete set of Kuznets/panic cycles. Cycle peaks occurred in 1818, 1836, 1854, 1872, 1890, 1907, 1925, 1951, 1969, and 1980. Troughs were observed in 1798, 1819, 1842, 1857, 1877, 1896, 1917, 1933, 1958, 1971, and 1991. The spacing between peaks or troughs varies from 11 to 26 years, with an average of 18-19 years.

The relation between the cycles

Table 2.2 summarizes the cycle dating described above. Prior to 1933, the minor cycles are business cycles. After 1933 the minor cycles are bull/bear cycles. Four bull/bear cycles, those corresponding to bear market troughs in 1934, 1960, 1980, and 1984, are skipped for reasons that will become clear in the next section. The 1805 bear market bottom (Table B.1) in between the 1798 and 1819 Kuznets troughs and the 1787 Kondratiev trough are assumed to be Juglar bottoms. Finally the K-cycle dating is added. All cycle troughs are expressed in terms of the closest recession bottom. That is, Kondratiev, Kuznets and Juglar bottoms are defined to be co-incident with a minor cycle bottom, making these cycles whole number multiples of minor cycles.

The industrial era business cycles and the bull/bear and short business cycles after 1933 have been interpreted as Kitchin cycles. Thus, the minor cycles after 1885 in Table 2.2 can be considered as Kitchin cycles. Business cycles during the pre-industrial era are not assigned to any class of cycle.

Table 2.2 shows that anywhere from 1 to 4 minor (business) cycles could fall within a Juglar during the pre-industrial era. That is, the lengths of business cycles could vary from 0.25 Juglar to 1.0 Juglar with an average of 0.56 Juglar. The shortest actual business cycle observed over this time was 2.5 years, about 0.25 of a standard 10 year Juglar. The longest was 9 years, which occupied a full Juglar. If business cycles were of random length between 0.25 and 1.0 Juglar, they would average around 0.62 Juglars, not too different from the observed average of 0.56. The standard deviation of the lengths of such random cycles would be equal to 35% of their average length. In actuality, the standard deviation of cycle length was 35% of average length. What this suggests is that before industrialization the shortest *natural* cycle was the Juglar at about 10 years. Shorter fluctuations were of essentially random length, except for the requirement that they be bound by a Juglar cycle.

Compare this to the situation after 1885. The standard deviation of business cycle lengths over 1885-1933 was only 22% of the average length, a tight dispersion indicative of a non-random cycle. Of course, business cycles after 1885 were not random; they reflected the Kitchin inventory cycle. The shortest natural cycle was now the Kitchin, which fixed business cycle length into a narrow range around 40 months. A fairly consistent relation of 3 or 4 Kitchin cycles per Juglar arose. After 1933, business cycles fell into two groups, one reflecting a slightly longer Kitchin cycle of about 4 years and the other a nine year Juglar cycle.

Table 2.2. Relation between Kondratiev, Kuznets, Juglar and minor cycles

Kondratiev Cycle	Kuznets Cycle	Juglar Cycle	Minor Cycles	Kondratiev Cycle	Kuznets Cycle	Juglar Cycle	Minor Cycles[1]
1787 T		1787	1787	1908	con't	1908	1908
		1798	1793	(K-summer)	1914		1911
(upwave)	1798	1798-1805	1798	1914	1914	1921	1914
		1805	1805	1921 P			1919
			1809	1921 P		1921	1921
1816 P			1812	(K-fall)			1924
1816 P	1819	1819	1816	1933	1933	1933	1927
	1819	1819-1829	1819	1933	1933		1932
(downwave)		1829	1829			1938	1938
1843T	1843	1843	1838	(K-winter)		1945	1942
1843 T	1843	1843-1849	1843	1949 T			1946
	1858	1849	1849	1949 T	1958		1949
(upwave)	1858	1858	1855		1958		1953
1867P		1858	1858	(K-spring)			1957
1867 P		1867	1861	1966	1970	1961	1962
	1879	1867	1867	1966	1970	1970	1966
	1879	1879	1870	(K-summer)		1975	1970
(downwave)		1879-1885	1879	1982 P		1982[2]	1974
		1885	1885	1982 P	1991	1982	1978
			1888	(K-fall)	1991	1991	1982
1897 T			1890		1990	1991	1987
1897 T	1897	1897	1893	2002			1990
(K-spring)	1897	1897	1897	2002		2001?	1994
1908			1900	2002-18?	2010?	2001?	1998
	con't	1908	1903	(K-winter)	↓	↓	2002
							2006?

[1]   The bear markets in 1934, 1960, 1980 and 1984 are skipped for reasons given in the next section.

[2]   The 1980 and 1982 recessions are treated as one double-dip recession

Using the data in Table 2.2 one can calculate the average length of the other cycles for all three eras. The Kuznets cycle length has been about 18 years long on average throughout the entire period. Since 1885 it has contained 3-5 Kitchin cycles. There has been no obvious relationship between the Kuznets and Kondratiev cycle. Table 2.2 shows a 2:1 relation between Juglar cycles and Kuznets cycles that ran throughout the entire 19th century. In the early 20th century the two cycles became uncoupled. The Panic of 1907, which produced a severe recession that marked a Juglar bottom, was the first financial panic that was not immediately followed by a major decline in real estate activity or valuation. There was instead a gradual drop in values and activity, which bottomed during WW I, well before the next Juglar bottom in 1921.

The Kondratiev cycle was unchanged at 53-54 years for both the pre-industrial and industrial periods. Cycle length has increased to about 72 years in the regulated period. A clear relation between the Juglar and Kondratiev cycles is not apparent. Table 2.2 shows 5 or 6 Juglars per Kondratiev during the pre-industrial era. No relation can be determined in the regulated era. There is some evidence for a relation between the Juglar and the K-season over the 1897-1933 period. The 1897-1908, 1908-1921 and 1921-33 Juglars roughly correspond to Kondratiev spring, summer and fall, suggesting that four Juglars per Kondratiev might have been an emergent pattern after industrialization, but such a K-cycle would be only 48 years long, a bit on the short side. The number of Kitchin cycles per K-cycle appears to have been 14 during the industrial era and 17 during the regulated era. Table 2.3 summarizes all these observations.

Table 2.3. Changing structure of socioeconomic cycles over the three eras

Cycle	Pre-industrial	Industrial	Regulated
Saeculum	~100 years (two K-cycles)	80-90 years (uncoupled from K-cycle)	72 years (one K-cycle)
K-cycle	1/2 saeculum; 5-6 Juglar	4 Juglar?	~72 years (one saeculum)
Generation	1/2 K-cycle; 1/4 saeculum	20-22 years (uncoupled from K-cycle)	~18 years (one K-season)
K-wave/Stock Cycle	1/2 K-cycle	2 Juglar?	~36 years
Kuznets cycle	~18 years (2 Juglar)	~18 years	~18 years
Juglar cycle	~10 yrs (1-4 bus cycles)	~12 years (one K-season)	~9 years (1/2 K-season?)
Kitchin cycle	N/A	1 bus cycle (~40 mo)	Bull/bear cycle (~4 yr)

The SMECT system of nested cycles

The market researcher Robert Bronson (2002) recently presented an intriguing scheme for connecting the K-cycle with shorter business cycles which he calls the Stock-Market and Economic Cycles Template or SMECT. SMECT starts with the Kitchin cycle as the fundamental building block of larger cycles. SMECT is primarily focused on the stock market rather than the economy and Kitchin cycles are defined by the periodicity of bear markets rather than by business cycles. Higher order cycles are defined as twice the next lower cycle. Thus, a Juglar cycle is two Kitchin cycles and a Kuznets cycle is two Juglar cycles. The Kuznets cycle is considered identical to the K-season or secular trend (see Table 2.4).

Thus, one can count three bull/bear (Kitchin) cycles in the secular bull market era (K-spring) from 1896-1907: 1896-1900, 1900-1903 and 1903-1907. Similarly, there are four bull/bear cycles in the 1907-1920 K-summer period, four bull/bear cycles in the 1920-1933 K-fall period and four bull/bear cycles in the 1933-1949 K-winter period (see Table B.1 in Appendix B) for a total of 15 Kitchin cycles in the 1896-1949 K-cycle. Note: the 1934 bear market was not counted for reasons that will be discussed below. Fifteen Kitchin cycles per Kondratiev is close to the 16 expected from SMECT (Table 2.4).

It must be stressed that the *stock market* cycles called Kitchin, Juglar and Kuznets in SMECT are *not* the same as the *economic* cycles of the same names described in the previous section. For example, the 1897-1907 period is described as a Juglar economic cycle in Table 2.2, but is a Kuznets stock market cycle in SMECT. Bronson points out that the idea that 16 Kitchin cycles make up one Kondratiev is consistent with the traditional length of the K-cycle of 53 years and the standard length of the Kitchin cycle of 40 months. That is, sixteen 40-month cycles span about 53 years.

Table 2.4. The SMECT scheme of nested binary cycles.

Cycle	Length
Kitchin	bull/bear cycle
Juglar	2 Kitchins
Kuznets	2 Juglars, 4 Kitchins
BAAC supercycle*	2 Kuznets, 4 Juglars, 8 Kitchins
Kondratiev cycle	2 Supercycles, 4 Kuznets, 8 Juglars, 16 Kitchins

* A BAAC supercycle is analogous to the Stock Cycle.

Although the larger cycles in SMECT are formally defined as geometric series multiples of Kitchin cycles, the larger cycles are not without auxiliary meanings. For example, the recessions of 1908, 1914, and 1921 (respective unemployment of 8.0%, 8.5% & 11.7%) were more severe than the neighboring recessions in 1904, 1911 and 1919 (respective unemployment 5.4%, 6.7% and 1.4%). The latter are just Kitchin troughs, while the former are also Juglar troughs. The 1908 recession is even more special, as it was associated one of the recurrent financial panics. This recession was also a Kuznets bottom. Finally, the 1897 and 1921 recession bottoms were the most severe of them all. These recessions marked an even higher-order change: the Kondratiev trough and peak, respectively. Similarly, the 1933 and 1921 recessions were by far the worst of the 1920's era and marked Kuznets bottoms. The 1942 bear market was larger (Table B.1) than either the 1938 and 1946 events showing the effect of the Juglar cycle.

Bronson advances the idea that with the onset of government economic management, the Kitchin cycle expanded from 40 months to four years in length, reflecting an emergent alignment between Kitchin-type business cycles and the four year electoral cycle. This is not a new idea. It has long been observed that business cycles show a correlation with the four-year electoral cycle. For example, 14 of the 21 bear market troughs since 1933 (Table B.1) fall in non-Presidential election years. The probability of this arising from chance is 0.001%, providing strong evidence for an election-linked four year cycle in the stock market. The correlation between election and business cycles is thought to reflect government economic management designed to help re-elect the party in power.

What *is* new is the idea that this new alignment not only increased the Kitchen cycle from 40 to 48 months, but also affected much longer cycles. Specifically, the Kondratiev cycle length increases from about 53 to 64 years. Thus, the SMECT model presents an explanation for Kondratiev cycle lengthening as well as providing an elegant categorization of the cycle structure of the 1896-1949 K-cycle.

Proceeding beyond the 1949 Kondratiev trough, one can count the number of bear markets that occurred during the 1949-1966 secular bull market (also a Kuznets cycle in SMECT). Consulting Table B.1, one counts five bear markets instead of the four expected from SMECT. However, using the strong correlation between the electoral cycle and the stock bull and bear markets, a good case can be made for mid-term elections (like 2002) acting as "bear market attractors" (Bronson, 2002). Bear markets that occur in Presidential election years should then be ignored as spurious, in which case the bear market bottoms in 1932, 1960, 1980 and 1984 should be ignored. Of course, the bear market bottom in 1932 is simply too large to be ignored, and since it happened before the rise of regulation, it *should* be included. In this case, the 1934 bottom should then be skipped because it occurred too close to the 1932 bottom to be part of a four year cycle. This is why the 1934, 1960, 1980, and 1984 bear markets were skipped in Table 2.2. In this case there are only 4 bull/bear cycles in the 1949-1966 Kuznets cycle and also 4 bear markets in the 1966-1982 Kuznets cycle. Thus, the first half of the current Kondratiev cycle also conforms to SMECT.

Here the power of the SMECT model is shown by its ability to bridge the transition for the industrial era to the regulated era. The explanatory pattern seen in the earlier cycles remains as well. For example, the average bear market severity (as assessed by equation 2.1) was greater in for the Juglar bottoms in 1958, 1966, 1974 and 1982 (average value of 3.0) than it was for the Kitchin bottoms in 1954, 1962, 1970, and 1978 (average value of 1.7). Similarly, the recessions associated with the Juglar bottoms showed greater severity (average unemployment 8.4%) than those associated with only a Kitchin bottom (average unemployment 5.9%).

There is a problem in the post-1982 period, however. Counting off-year election bear markets for the 1982-2002 secular bull market period (Kondratiev fall) gives five rather than the four expected from SMECT. The problem comes from the 20-year length of this Kondratiev fall season instead of the 16 years expected from SMECT. Bronson resolves this problem by setting the end of the recent BAAC Supercycle bull market (and beginning of Kondratiev winter) in 1997 when the equally-weighted stock index began its secular bear market, instead of 2000, the nominal peak in the major capitalization-weighted indices (Bronson, 2002). In this way 1998 becomes the Kuznets cycle bottom, equivalent to 1932 in the last K-cycle. But this assignment makes the recent bear market (the worst of the current K-cycle) simply a reflection of a Kitchin cycle by itself. It destroys the alignment in which more severe events are generally associated with the troughs of higher-order cycles. Setting 2002 and 1990 as Juglar bottoms preserves this, but leaves three Kitchins in the most recent Juglar cycle—in violation of the SMECT structure.

An argument can be made that economic policymaker intervention has shifted the effects of the onset of Kondratiev winter forward from 1998 (when they should have occurred) to now. No such intervention occurred for the last cycle and so the 1929-1932 equivalent decline is playing out one Kitchin cycle later than it normally would in the absence of policymaker interventions. This argument is a "cycle lengthening" argument, but SMECT already accounts for cycle lengthening though Kitchin cycle expansion. Further delays by policymakers *should already be part* of any model for the post-1933 economy, when such interventions are now normal. Thus, SMECT's failure to account for the extension of the boom beyond 1998 is a problem.

Another feature of the SMECT model not yet discussed is that the lower order cycles are necessarily in phase with the longer cycles. That is, a BAAC Supercycle turning point (like 1998) is necessarily also a turning point in all the lower-order cycles (Kuznets, Juglar and Kitchin). The empirically derived cycles shown in Table 2.2 do not support this alignment. Of course, the SMECT cycles do not refer to the economic phenomenon associated with the cycles of the same name, they are simply names used to classify cycles composed of geometric multiples of Kitchin cycles—which do have a mechanistic interpretation in SMECT (they follow the four-year electoral cycle). On the other hand, the higher order cycles do have meaning. Sixteen Kitchins are supposed to define a K-cycle, which can be independently assessed by long-term trends in monetary variables like interest rates. Eight Kitchins are supposed to define a BAAC supercycle and four a secular stock market trend, both of which can be independently assessed using measures like Tobin's Q. The only cycle in SMECT which does not have a specific independent meaning is the Juglar cycle. The Juglar in SMECT does *not* correspond with the longer category of business cycles since 1933. The Juglar troughs in 1998, 1966 and 1942 fall into the middle of the 1990's, 1960's and WW II business cycles rather than align with their troughs.

The generational interpretation of economic cycles

As an alternative to SMECT, I present the generational scheme shown in Table 2.5. The same four-year Kitchin cycles found in SMECT are retained. However no fixed connection between these cycles and the longer ones is assumed. Although each longer cycle will necessarily contain a whole number of Kitchin cycles this number is not necessarily constant. The organizing principle behind these cycles is Strauss and Howe's generational cycle, or more specifically the modern incarnation of this cycle with 18-year generations that I presented in Chapter One. Prior to around 1820, turnings had been longer, reflecting generations of biological length. The biological generational length has a natural basis in human reproduction, whereas the 18-year length is artificial. It cannot even be related to phase of life as Strauss and Howe do with their idea of 22-year generations.

Table 2.5. Comparison of SMECT with generational scheme for the regulated era

Cycle	SMECT (w/o generations)	Generational scheme
Bull/Bear market cycle	4 years (same as Kitchin)	4 yrs (same as Kitchin)
Business cycle	Kitchin or Juglar	Kitchin or Juglar
Kitchin	4 years (electorally-based short business cycle)	4 years (same as SMECT)
Juglar	8 years (2 Kitchins)	9 yrs avg (long business cycle, 1/2 K-season, *usually* 2 Kitchins)
Kuznets cycle	16 years (4 Kitchins)	18 yrs—not same as K-season
Kondratiev season	Same as Kuznets cycle	18 years—1 psychological generation
Supercycle/Stock Cycle	32 years (1/2 of K-cycle)	36 years—2 psychological generations
Kondratiev Cycle/Saeculum	64 years—no relation to saeculum	72 years—4 psychological generations

The 18-year generation can be related to the Kondratiev season, the Kuznets cycle and to the political cycle identified by the American historian Arthur Schlesinger (1949). Schlesinger proposed a cyclical concept of American politics in which the political "spirit of the times", or *zeitgeist*, oscillated between "liberal" and "conservative" eras every 16 years on average. He had some notable success in predicting shifts in his political cycle. In 1924, he predicted that Coolidge-style conservatism would last until 1932. In 1939, he predicted that the liberal mood would end in about 1947. In 1949, he predicted a shift to liberalism in 1962 and a shift back to conservatism in 1978 (Goertzel, 2000). Table 2.6 compares Schlesinger political cycles, Kuznets cycles, K-seasons, and the alternate turnings I presented in Table 1.2. The first three turnings align with Kondratiev *waves* (half K-cycles) in accordance with the pre-industrial pattern shown in Table 2.3. The last four turnings are aligned with Kondratiev *seasons* (quarter K-cycles). These seven turnings are identical to those proposed by Strauss and Howe. I also note that the first three turnings in Table 2.6 also are aligned with the Kuznets cycles and that roughly four Kuznets cycles fall into the 1860-1929 period when turnings were transforming from alignment with Kondratiev waves to alignment with Kondratiev seasons. My alternate turnings were drawn to align with the Kuznets cycle and thus continue the same pattern that had emerged in the three turnings before the Civil War. These alternate turnings allow for a Civil War Hero generation and thus eliminate the problematic Civil War anomaly.

As I described in *The Kondratiev Cycle*, there was no clear relation between political cycles and the K-cycle during the 19th century. Before 1840 and after 1920, political cycles were aligned with Kondratiev seasons. In between there was no apparent relation. An emergent relationship between Kuznets/real estate cycles and political cycle can be identified by noting that each political era between the War of 1812 and the Civil War had its own real estate boom and subsequent bust. Following the shift from liberal to conservative in 1816 there followed a land boom which peaked in 1818 and was followed by the Panic of 1819, the first of what would become a regularly-recurring feature of the American economy. The 1820's were a depressionary decade which saw the liberals under Andrew Jackson make two attempts (1824 and 1828) at ousting the conservatives. The second was successful, marking the next shift in the political cycle in 1829. Shortly afterward a new land boom began which peaked in 1836 and was followed by the Panic of 1837. The country fell into a deep depression, which marked the Kondratiev trough. It also brought about another political shift in 1841. This cycle also had its own real estate boom, which peaked in 1854 and was followed by the Panic of 1857. The next election saw yet another shift with the election of Abraham Lincoln, champion of the new Republican party.

Lincoln's untimely death and his replacement by his unpopular vice president, who was a Democrat, resulted in an early shift in political zeitgest. This shortened cycle lacked a real estate boom. The cycle which followed enjoyed its own boom, which peaked in 1872 and was followed by the Panic of 1873. The election of 1876 was another deal-brokered affair like that the election of 1824. Democrat Tilden may have beaten Republican Hayes, but an election commission comprised of a majority of Republicans assigned the victory to Hayes. After the election, the economy began to improve, not because of another real estate boom, but because of the railroad boom associated with the Kondratiev-aligned innovation wave. Thus, the economy recovered from the depression induced by the Panic of 1873, and there was no replay of 1828 in 1880 (Tilden declined to run). As a result there was no political shift and the conservative era began by Grant's inauguration in 1869 continued to another real estate peak and subsequent panic in 1893. The 1896 election is considered by political scientists to be one of the periodic "critical elections" that produce lasting re-alignments in political power. The Democratic challenger was again defeated as in 1876 and it seemed the post-Civil War conservative era would continue on for yet another Kuznets cycle. But McKinley was not cut from the same cloth as his conservative predecessors and his vice president (who succeeded him after his death in 1901) was an outright progressive. Thus, a period of liberal zeitgeist actually emerged in the aftermath of the 1896 election.

The early 20th century saw the weakening of the Kuznets cycle. There was no major depression or real estate collapse following the "rich man's panic" in 1907 and no change in political zeitgeist. The swing to conservatism didn't occur until 1919 as the nation yearned for a return to normalcy after the tumultuous war years. The political cycle had become decoupled from land value and the Kuznets cycle (a barometer of the old agricultural economy), in favor of the stock market and the Stock Cycle (a barometer of the new industrial economy). The conservative era of the 1920's neatly encompassed the secular bull market in stocks, and with the bull market's end came the shift to liberalism in 1931. Like the political cycle, turnings ceased to follow the Kuznets cycle and instead began to follow the Stock Cycle around this time. After 1929, turnings, K-seasons and political cycles have all been aligned (see Table 2.6). This shift reflected a new interaction between generations, the political cycle, and the K-cycle that transformed the nature of all of them.

Table 2.6 Comparison of Kuznets cycles with turnings and political eras

K-seasons	Kuznets Cycle[1]	Political era[2]	Turnings
1787-1802 (spring)		1788-1801 (C)	
1802-1816 (summer)		1801-1816 (L)	Era of Good Feelings (1794-18221)
1816-1836 (fall)	1818 peak	1816-1829 (C)	
1836-1843 (winter)	1836 peak	1829-1841 (L)	Transcendental Awakening (1822-1844)
1843-1864 (upwave)	1843-1858	1841-1861 (C)	Mexican War & Sectionalism (1844-1860)
1864-1897 (downwave)	1858-1879	1861-1869 (L)	Civil War & Reconstruction (1860-1877)
1897-1908 (spring)	1879-1897	1869-1901 (C)	Reconstruction & Gilded Age (1877-1894)
1908-1921 (summer)	1897-1914	1901-1919 (L)	Third Great Awakening (1894-1912)
1921-1933 (fall)	1914-1933	1919-1931 (C)	World War I & Prohibition (1912-1929)
1933-1949 (winter)	1933-1958	1931-1947 (L)	Depression & World War II (1929-1946)
1949-1966 (spring)	1958-1971	1947-1963 (C)	American High (1946-1964)
1966-1982 (summer)	1971-1991	1963-1980 (L)	Consciousness Revolution (1964-1982)
1982-2000 (fall)	1991-	1980-2000? (C)	Culture Wars (1982-2001)

[1] Cycles are trough-to-trough unless otherwise indicated
[2] The letters C and L denote conservative and liberal eras, respectively

How the 18-year Stock Cycle and 72-year K-cycle emerged

The rise of the industrial economy did more than simply introduce the Kitchin cycle. It also increased the intensity of the Kuznets cycle, which had already been part of the pre-industrial economy. Thus, while the Kuznets-related Panic of 1819 was the first panic to make it into the history books, it was a pretty mild bear market. The Panic of 1837 was worse and the one in 1857 worse yet. The Panic of 1873 ushered in the second worst bear market of all time. The depression following the Panic of 1893 was the worst up to that time. This depression was the first to take place with a majority of the population involved in non-agricultural occupations. Although hard times on the farm were a frequent occurrence, depressions did not usually mean hunger. Yet for the large numbers of urban workers thrown onto "the industrial scrap heap" the depression of the 1890's produced a level of suffering unprecedented for a business fluctuation.

Despite the severity of the depression, little government action was taken. President Cleveland resisted pressure to provide relief with expanded public works programs, as did many in Congress. Senator James Berry of Arkansas, voicing the dominant mind-set, declared that "It is not the purpose of this government to give work to individuals throughout the United States by appropriating money which belongs to other people and does not belong to the Senate" (Furfero, 2000). Power was still held by the Gilded generation, the last to come of age in a pre-industrial America. This generation was still steeped in the Jeffersonian concept of America as a nation of sturdy yeoman individualists, who rejected the sort of collectivist politics then popular in Europe.

Yet the very next panic in 1907, although considerably milder in its effects, brought reform in the guise of the Federal Reserve System. The Progressive generation then in power had come of age in the midst of industrialization, and was more cognizant of the new realities of industrial America. The Progressive reforms occurred during the 1901-19 period of liberal zeitgeist. It was followed by a speculative conservative era. As it turned out, the Progressive reforms were not enough to prevent the stock market crash and depression in 1929-33. The depression triggered the Crisis turning, the first time a business cycle downturn had done so. Crisis eras produce massive changes in society, and this one was no different. The generation in power, the Missionary (b 1874-90) was the first completely industrial generation. The response they crafted to the problems of the Great Depression (Keynesian economics) and the dictators it produced (WW II) completely transformed the role of government in the economy, producing a lengthened Kondratiev cycle now fully aligned with the generational saeculum cycle.

It was a change in the interaction between political and economic cycles that produced the increase in K-cycle length. During the 19th century the Schlesinger political cycle had been intertwined with the Kuznets cycle as described earlier. Schlesinger cycles can be thought of as cycles of domestic rent-seeking politics. Rent seeking is a term economists use to refer to actions designed to produce economic outcomes different from what would occur from action of market forces alone, usually to the benefit of a politically powerful special interest. An example of how political rent-seeking intermeshes with economics would be the Graduation Act of 1854, which slashed the price of government lands unsold for a long time by 90%. This fire sale of public lands ignited an explosion of land speculation. Not surprisingly, 1854 shows up as one of the Kuznets peaks in real-estate speculation, occurring precisely 18 years after the previous peak in 1836.

The Kuznets cycle was a domestic economic cycle reflecting periodic booms and busts in land values. Such cycles were the dominant factor in the domestic economy until industrialization had progressed to a very great extent. They did not affect the monetary environment, however, which was the realm of the Kondratiev cycle. Thus, Schlesinger-type *domestic* political cycles interacted with the Kuznet cycle to produce an 18-year cycle in the *domestic* political economy, but *not* the monetary environment.

The Kondratiev cycle was aligned with the war/hegemony cycle, which is a cycle of *international* politics. The Kondratiev cycle is a cycle in the *international* economy, which mostly reflects monetary factors such as prices, debt and interest rates. Kondratiev peaks reflected major government expenditures for "peak wars" that produced massive indebtedness which affected prices and interest rates before, during, and long after the peak war period.

After 1933, the Federal government began to engage in "war-like" deficit spending during peacetime in order to affect the economy, much as a war does. That is, an artificial "war spending cycle" (i.e. Kondratiev cycle) was superimposed upon the economy to fight cyclic depressions in response to a domestic political mandate. Thus, the war-spending cycle stopped following the war/hegemonic cycle, and started to follow the Schlesinger political cycle. The K-cycle followed the shift in spending, now becoming based on 18-year "political generations" in place of the old cycle based on 27-year biologically-based "war-cycle generations".

The first indication of how the saeculum and the associated Schlesinger political cycle were now controlling the economic cycles (instead of the other way around) appeared during the High (1946-64). The High was a conservative era, yet the emphasis was on the tenets of fiscal conservatism, balanced budgets and financial probity, even at the cost of maintaining the high tax rates from WW II. Although conservative politics tends to tolerate speculation as a necessary side effect of wealth creation, the *style* of economic management during the High was not conducive to speculation. As a result, the post-war High was free of anything resembling a panic and the Kuznets cycle was muted. The secular bull market from 1949-1966 ended at the *lowest* valuation level of any secular bull market, showing the depressed "animal spirits" of the time. According to the generational model, the fiscally conservative policies and financial self restraint of the 1950's was a natural consequence of the generational peer-personalities of the adult generations: cautious, risk-adverse Nomad elders, team-playing, disciplined Heroes as mature adults, and compliant twenty-something Artists.

Business cycles continued to be aligned with periodic bear markets as they had been before 1933, except the period between them had increased to four years, in accordance with the SMECT model. As the High gave way to the Awakening, things "loosened up" financially and speculative forces began to stir.

By the 1970's, "self-expression" and the rise of the individualistic ethic (coming with the arrival of a new generation of Prophets) encouraged deficit spending, tax revolts and speculation alongside sex, drugs and rock 'n roll. Strauss and Howe call such periods Awakening turnings. They are times when "people stop believing that social progress requires social discipline" and develop "a high tolerance for risk-prone lifestyles" (Strauss and Howe, 1997b). People disdain the prosperity and security of a High, though covertly they are taken for granted. The development of the Awakening mirrored a political shift from conservative to liberal as well as an erosion of financial rectitude. Taxes were cut in the early 1960's and the decision to finance the Vietnam War through deficit spending rather than increased taxes contributed to an inflationary environment that would make speculation more attractive in the 1970's. War stimulus was probably responsible for extension the 1960's expansion beyond 1966, when it should have ended according to SMECT.

Kondratiev spring ended in 1966, just two years after the beginning of the Awakening, as indicated by the beginning of a secular bear market. Yet economic good times continued until 1973. The credit crunch in 1966 failed to bring on a recession; economic conditions remained favorable for the first half of Kondratiev summer. On the other hand, the 1966 bear market signaled a shift to a highly speculative era seeing first the "go-go years" of the late 1960's and then the "nifty-fifty" era of the early 1970's. This same period also saw the re-emergence of a full-blown Kuznets cycle. The persistence of good times over the 1966-1973 period reflected the efforts of government policy makers to maintain full employment using Keynesian stimulus in the face of Kondratiev summer. It worked for a while, but the eventual result was stagflation.

The experience of stagflation did not lead to an abandonment of government economic management, but rather to a change in management style. Liberal Keynesian fiscal management was dropped in favor of conservative supply-side monetary management. This shift mirrored a shift in zeitgeist from liberal to conservative, the Reagan Revolution. Another interpretation of this era is what Strauss and Howe call an Unraveling turning. The Unraveling "begins as a society-wide embrace of the liberating cultural forces set loose by the Awakening". People "vigorously assert an ethos of pragmatism, self-reliance, laissez faire, and national (or sectional or ethnic) chauvinism" (Strauss and Howe, 1997b).

In the early 1980's, the Federal Reserve, under its new monetarist focus, hiked interest rates to their highest level in the history of the United States, breaking the back of inflation. Taxes were cut substantially again, especially those for capital gains, and as inflation subsided, a great bull market in stocks ensued. This policy had the same effect as that during the early 1920's when the decline of WW I inflation, a capital gains tax cut, and a belief that the Fed had made financial panics a thing of the past unleashed speculative forces. The 1920-29 secular bull market is cycle-equivalent to that in 1982-2000. The secular bull market peak in 2000 had the *highest* valuation level in history, showing extremely powerful animal spirits—exactly the reverse of the previous secular bull market peak.

The speculative spirit reborn in the Awakening had become sanctioned by official policy during the Unraveling. For example, the 1987 stock market crash was met by copious liquidity, which allowed the market to recover its losses in just two years, resulting in extension of the already-long 1980's expansion to the next Kitchin cycle bottom. Congress passed a capital gains tax cut in 1997 in order to stimulate further stock price increases in an already overvalued market. The next year the Fed executed a well-timed surprise rate cut that ignited an explosive stock rise that was even more extreme than the late 1920's blow-off. Both of these policies served to extend the already long 1990's business cycle by one more Kitchin, and as a result Kondratiev fall was extended well beyond its length in previous cycles. The net result of these various interventions has been to subtly increase the length of the K-cycle from the 64-year length called for by SMECT to a 72-year length fully aligned with the saeculum.

The timing of the K-cycle and its sub-harmonics the Stock Cycle and K-season shifted from the biological generation of the war/hegemonic cycle to the 18-year generation associated with the Schlesinger cycles. This 18-year generation was already present long before 1933. The Kuznets cycle, cast adrift from saeculum after 1933, continued on, still showing an (average) 18 year cycle length, but now unaligned with the other cycles. The significance of this will be seen in the next section.

What the cycles have to say about this secular bear market

So far, I have presented a summary of three economic cycles that operate at a shorter scale than the Stock Cycle. The cycles were dated and evidence supplied to support the dating. Two models were presented that attempt to explain how the cycles have evolved over time. I favor the generational model, which posits that the fundamental length in the modern system of economic cycles is 18 years. The clearest recent demonstration of this length was the 18-year secular bull market from 1982 to 2000. Based on this fundamental length, I forecast that the secular bear market that began in 2000 will last until around 2018.

The 18-year fundamental length also shows up in the historical length of the Kuznets real estate cycle. The real estate-based Kuznets cycle has never been in phase with the K-cycle, as is the 16-year stock-based "Kuznets cycle" in SMECT (see Figure 2.5). This remains true today. Thus, the Kuznets cycle can exert effects independently of the K-cycle, sometimes adding to the Kondratiev trend and other times opposing it. Hence, the 2000-2002 slump, although "K-cycle equivalent" to 1929-1932, is not as severe as even the mild 1990 recession because it lacks a real-estate (Kuznets) cycle downturn. That is, the Kuznets cycle at present is acting in opposition to the K-cycle, moderated what would otherwise be a serious economic slump.

One might point out that the current (Fall, 2002) strength in real estate reflects the twelve rate cuts made by the Federal Reserve since the beginning of 2001. But these twelve rate cuts have done nothing to prevent the stock market from falling 35% since they began. The stock market fell because it had gotten too overvalued, that is, it had reached its peak in the Stock Cycle and thus had to start coming down, regardless of what the Fed did. On the other hand, real estate valuation has not reached extreme levels. That is, the Kuznets peak has yet to be reached, so real estate can continue to rise in valuation.

It has been 22 years since the last McFadden price peak in 1980, so another one is overdue. The recent rise in existing housing prices in Figure 2.5 suggests that we may have entered the boom stage that marks the final approach to a Kuznets peak. The data in Figure 2.5 is not consistent with the idea that housing is particularly overvalued in November 2002, however. For both existing and new houses, prices relative to income are well below the levels reached at previous real estate peaks in the late 1970's and 1980's, respectively. Existing home prices would have to rise another 10% relative to income for valuations to reach late 1970's levels. This level would be reached in a couple of years if current trends continue, implying a Kuznets real estate peak around 2004. This would give a ~24 year length for this Kuznets cycle, which is on the long side. The cycle before the present one (1969-80) was unusually short, however, so the average length of the two most recent cycles has remained close to the 18 year expected length. Applying the 18-year standard spacing to the last trough in 1992 projects the next Kuznets trough for around 2010. What this says is real estate is not in a bubble (as of November 2002) and should *not* collapse in the coming months and years.

Since real estate has not yet reached its cycle maximum, rate cuts have supported real estate, just as they did for stocks in 1998. By around 2004 we may well have reached a Kuznets peak, after which Fed rate cuts would be ineffective in preventing a real estate bust in a future recession. This interpretation suggests that the current downturn is largely stock market driven, being the result of the inevitable downturn following a peak in long-term stock market valuation (P/R). Indeed, current weakness almost entirely comes from weak business investment spending, reflecting the poor business outlook generated by continuing weakness in the stock market. Consumer demand has remained strong. Thus no double-dip recession is to be expected and the stock market may well rally over the next few years (after November 2002), in accordance with P/R valuation, as will be examined in the next chapter. The *next* recession will likely reflect major downturns in both stock market/business investment and real estate market/consumer spending.

Chapter 3

Stocks—What Three Valuation Methods Have to Say

This chapter examines three S&P500 valuation methods for what they have to say about the progress of the secular bear market that began in 2000. The first method is an averaged price to earnings ratio described by Robert Shiller in his book *Irrational Exuberance* (Shiller, 2000). The S&P500 index value is divided by the average index earnings over the previous 10 years. The price to earnings ratio (P/E) is probably the most widely used stock valuation measure. By averaging earnings over ten years, Shiller smooths out short-term fluctuations, revealing the long trend trends that define the Stock Cycle.

The second method examined is the Q ratio originally developed by the late Yale economics professor James Tobin. The Q ratio measures the ratio of the market value of factories and other corporate assets to their replacement cost. When Q is low, as it was in the late 1970's and early 1980's, companies tend to expand by acquiring other companies instead of building plants or buying equipment. When Q is high it makes better sense to build new assets directly. Obviously, if one can buy an asset more cheaply by buying the *stock* of the asset-owning company than buying the asset directly, the stock is undervalued. This is the basis of the use of Q as a measure of stock valuation. When Q rises much above one, stocks should be sold as being overvalued.

Tobin's original presentation of his ratio only covered one secular bull market peak, in which Q indeed reached a value just over one before beginning a long-term decline. Thus, advocates of this ratio would be warning of an overvalued market in late 1993 as Q was approaching one (Rothchild, 1998). The enormous rise in the market after 1994 served to decrease interest in Q. In their recent book, *Valuing Wall Street*, Smithers and Wright (2000) extend the record of Q back to 1900, covering three previous secular bull market peaks. They found the value of Q at the 1960's peak (1.06) was the lowest of the three, with the highest (1.35) occurring in 1929. Thus, markets tend to rise significantly above one at major market peaks and so the Q value just below one in late 1993 did not necessarily signal a top in 1994, stocks could well rise further.

Finally, I look at P/R, which I introduced in my book *Stock Cycles*. Business resources (R) are defined as the cumulative sum of S&P500 earnings less dividends paid out, all in terms of constant dollars. The stock index price (P) is also put into constant-dollar form, and the ratio P/R calculated. P/R is like Q in that it is an asset-based rather than earnings-based measure. The asset in this case (R) is the cumulative sum of constant-dollar retained earnings which can be thought of as a proxy for constant-dollar book value. The big difference between an ordinary book value and R is that the value added each year is adjusted to a constant dollar basis before being added onto R, while in a book value the values are expressed in nominal dollars. The idea behind the inflation adjustment is that earnings are invested in real assets that maintain their value against inflation. To the extent that the assets obtained using retained earnings are tangible things like plant and equipment, which have a replacement value, P/R should essentially measure the same thing as Q and show the same cycles.

Figure 3.1 shows a plot of P/R and Q since 1900. The two measures closely track each other as expected. There are a few differences; the most relevant to this discussion is the tendency for Q to be higher than P/R since 1990. Tobin's Q focuses on the replacement value of a company's assets (less liabilities) or net worth, as its measure of what the company is worth. This measure places stress on tangible assets, for which a replacement value can be obtained. Intangible assets, such as goodwill, are not counted. To the extent that earnings are used to purchase intangible assets, R captures intangibles. With the development of the "information economy", a greater impact of intangible assets on the value of the stock market is to be expected. It is reasonable to think that net worth underestimates the true value of a business, and that Q might be "reading high" today.

Figure 3.1 Tobin's Q and P/R during the 20th century

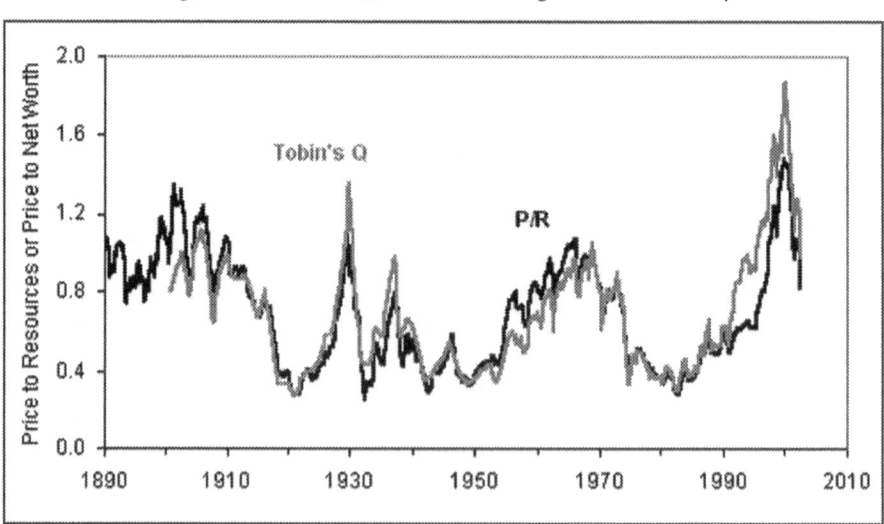

The behavior of different valuation methods in the recent secular bull market

The purpose of these valuation tools with respect to investment planning is to give an idea of where we are in the Stock Cycle. During a secular bull market, the goal is to remain fully invested until near the end of secular bull market, at which time one shifts to an alternate investment strategy. One does not wish to shift too soon, as the returns expected from alternate investments are likely to be much lower than those from stocks in a secular bull market. I have already discussed how the lack of a sufficiently-long history for Tobin's Q could have led some investors to a conclusion that the secular bull market was already nearing its end in 1993 and that stocks should be avoided after 1995. By expanding the history back to 1900, as Smithers and Wright have done, it is seen that Q values as high as 1.35 had been seen in the past, and might have been expected again. Thus investors following Q with an expanded historical record would have been less bearish in the early 1990's. Nevertheless, users of Q would still have already made their preparations for the coming secular bear market well before the third quarter of 1997 when Q reached its 1929 level.

Historical values for Shiller's P/E are available from 1881 on. Values between 17 and 32 have been seen at previous secular bull market peaks. Shiller's P/E rose above its previous all-time high of 32 in January 1997. Indeed, shortly following Shiller's presentation of his P/E model to the Federal Open Markets Committee in December 1996, Chairman Alan Greenspan gave his famous "irrational exuberance" speech, in which he cautioned investors about high stock valuations. Followers of Shiller's P/E valuation would have heeded the Chairman's warning and made preparations for a secular bear market at the end of 1996.

P/R had varied between 1.08 and 1.34 at previous secular bull market peaks. P/R also reached its previous all-time high, just like the other measures. But this occurred in January 1999, not in 1997. Thus a follower of P/R would have remained fully invested for an additional 1-2 years of bull market. But there was yet another advantage. In late summer 1997, Congress passed a capital gains tax cut. This act was intended to encourage investment—specifically the kind of investment that produces capital gains. That is, this act was intended to make stocks go up in price. On two prior occasions, (1921 and 1981) when capital gains taxes had been lowered to 20% or lower, a most satisfactory stock bull market had ensued afterward. So it seems that this sort of policy works. Thus, I had reason to believe that with the boost produced by the capital gains tax cut, the bull market should end at all-time high valuation levels. Hence I only started reducing my stock allocation below 100% in late 1998 and in January 1999 I was still 50% invested in stocks. I did not completely exit stocks in my 401K until September 3, 1999.

Figure 3.2 Shiller's P/E during secular bear markets

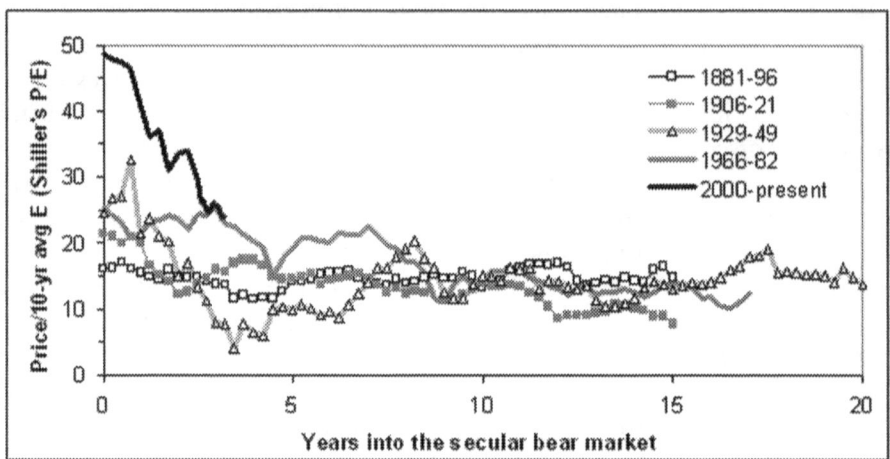

Of the three valuation tools, P/R reached record levels the latest, two years after Shiller's P/E and a year and a half after Tobin's Q. Significant stock gains occurred over these periods. But this may be merely a fluke. In order for P/R to be considered an effective valuation measure, it is necessary for it to give a proper signal for re-entry. In the next section, the three measures will be used to provide an assessment of the market's prospects as of its summer 2002 levels.

The behavior of different valuation methods in past secular bear markets

This section is based largely on commentary I wrote on August 25, 2002 in which I used the three valuation tools to assess the likelihood that a major stock low had been reached in July 2002 (Alexander, 2002e, 2002f). Here I will update this commentary through March 2003, showing what the three valuation measures have to say about the present secular bear market. Figure 3.2 shows a graph of Shiller's P/E for the present secular bear versus that for previous secular bear markets: 1881-96, 1906-21, 1929-49 and 1966-82. Several things are evident. The value of P/E at the beginning of the current secular bear market was *much* higher than that at the beginning of the previous bear markets. Since its 2000 peak Shiller's P/E has fallen dramatically, but it is still well above the levels it has seen at this stage in previous secular bear markets. The S&P500 would have to fall into the 400's for P/E to be within the historical range. Thus, advocates of this valuation method would caution against re-entry until after another 40% drop from the fall 2002 lows.

Figure 3.3 Tobins's Q during secular bear markets

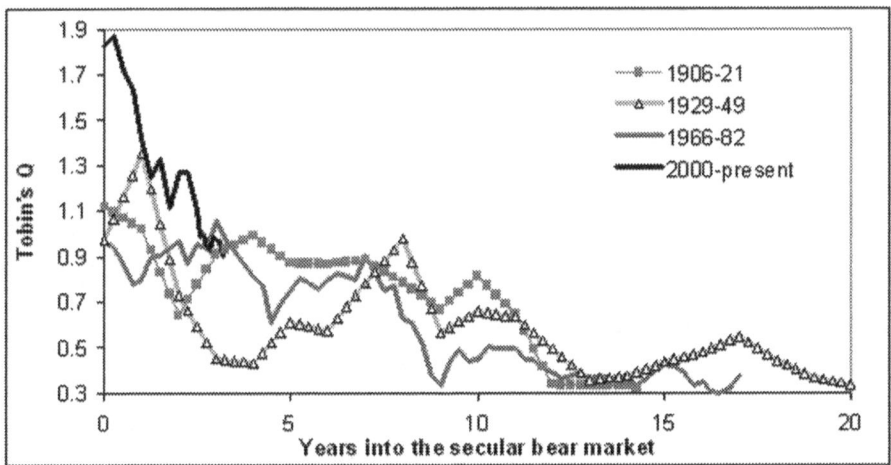

Figure 3.3 shows a graph of Tobin's Q for the current secular bear market and three previous ones. Similar observations can be made. As with P/E the level of Q reached in 2000 was way above any of its previous levels, but not quite as extreme as with P/E. Since its 2000 high, Q has also fallen dramatically. Like P/E it too is fairly high relative to its historical values in early stage secular bear markets. The S&P500 would have to fall to the 600's for Q to fall into its historical range in previous secular bear markets. Thus, advocates of Tobin's Q would caution against re-entry until after a 15% or greater drop from the fall 2002 lows.

Figure 3.4 shows a graph of P/R for the current secular bear market and the four previous ones. Like P/E and Q, P/R in 2000 was higher than it had ever been. But the margin of excess was less. Since its 2000 high, P/R has fallen like the other two measures. Unlike the other two measures, P/R in July 2002, October 2002 or March 2003 was not particularly high relative it its historical values in previous secular bear markets. It was not low either. Figure 3.4 shows that the 1932 low in P/R was far below today's levels, but that was during the

Great Depression. Assuming that no Depression occurs, an assumption supported by the Kuznets cycle in the last chapter and the monetary arguments to be made in the next chapter, the extreme low of 1932 should be ignored as not relevant to today. In this case the three other secular bear markets should provide the historical context. By mid-summer 2002, P/R had already fallen below the levels reached during the *first* bear market of all three of these secular bear markets. Lower levels than those today were obtained in the subsequent bear markets, and it is expected that P/R will decline well below its recent lows in future bear markets during this secular bear period.

Figure 3.4 P/R during secular bear markets

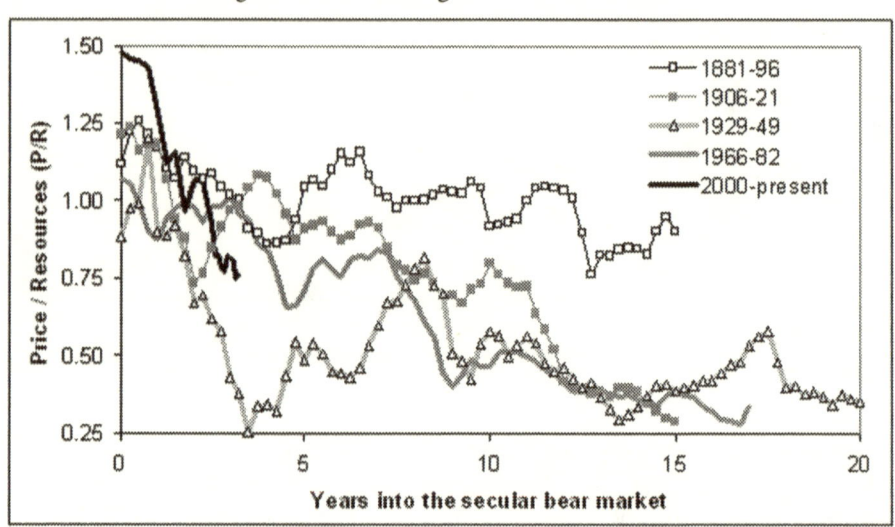

Thus, although the index certainly could continue to fall (and it has so far fallen to a marginal new low in October 2002 and a re-test of the summer lows in March 2003) and P/R would remain within its historical norms, it does not have too. Followers of P/R would not caution against re-entry at the lows in summer and fall 2002 or late winter 2003. I reached 80% stock allocation in my 401K in July 2002, indicating a fair degree of bullishness. A statistical assessment of future returns can be made much as was done in *Stock Cycles*. In September 2001 P/R reached 0.97 and by October 2002 it was 0.77. A projection can be made by calculating future five year capital gain returns and P/R for all months between 1871 and 1997. Those results with P/R between 0.77 and 0.97 were removed and ranked according to return and the returns at the various percentile levels noted. An estimated dividend yield of 1.8% was added to these capital gain data to give total return. These values would correspond to S&P500 purchases made in Sept 2001 or June 2002-present (March 2003).

I did this and the median total return obtained was 5.9%. To give an idea of risk, I note that 12% of the historical total returns were negative and about 30% of the total returns were less than that available from a money market fund. On the positive side, over 20% of the returns were double-digit. This exercise implies a 70% probability of beating the money market fund going forward from the summer-fall 2002 levels, with an expectation of nearly 6% return. Worst case is a 1 in 8 probability of losing money. The worst outcome amongst the 385 returns is a 60% loss of principal, while the best outcome is a 135% gain.

To put this into perspective, examination of the 70 returns for P/R above 1.15, which roughly corresponds to five-year investments made between November 1998 and June 2001, shows a median projected return of 0.8%. Nearly 60% of the sample shows returns less than current ~1% money market rates, and one-third show losses. None of the returns were double digit. The best result of the 70 is a 47% gain, while the worst is a 69% loss. Clearly, the environment for five year stock investments in late 2002/early 2003 is far better than it was in 1998 or 1999.

The current market provides a good test of the three valuation methods. Suppose the S&P500 fails to fall significantly below its October 9, 2002 close. If this happens, P/R will be the only valuation method that gave a green light to stock investments made on that date. On the other hand, suppose the S&P500 drops to an ultimate bottom below 550 *without* a deflationary depression. In this case, P/R valuation would be invalidated. Such a low level of P/R this early in a secular bear market has only occurred once, during the Great Depression. Were it to happen now without a depression would necessarily invalidate P/R as a useful measure. Shiller's P/E says such a development is to be *expected*, no depression is needed. Furthermore, Tobin's Q does not rule out sub-550 levels, only P/R does.

Suppose a subsequent decline takes the index to an ultimate bottom well below the October 9 close, but above 600 on the S&P 500? In this case, P/R would not be invalidated, but it would be Tobin's Q that did the best job. Shiller's P/E would still be invalidated. Finally a drop below 400 on the S&P500 without a depression would move Shiller's P/E into top place as best valuation model of the three. So here there is a real-life test of the three valuation methods. I expect to obtain an answer by the end of 2004.

Chapter 4

Monetary Implications for Stocks, Bonds and Gold

In this chapter, I will discuss the monetary environment to be expected based on our position within the Kondratiev cycle. A correct assessment of location with the cycle is required in order to do this, which is a lot harder to do than one might think. I gave a brief treatment of the Kondratiev Cycle in *Stock Cycles* in which I concluded that we were at the time of what I called the DG peak. This meant that we were about two-thirds of the way through the Kondratiev downwave, and that the coming secular bear market could end as soon as 2010. Since the secular bear market had not yet begun at that time (early 2000) it looked like it was going to be a short secular bear market. This idea was also consistent with the standard timing of the Kondratiev cycle of 50-60 years.

At that time, my assumption was that Kondratiev winter, or the secular bear market portion of the Kondratiev downwave, usually began at the DG peak. The 1929 event had been a fluke caused by an usually large "fall from plateau" (another Kondratiev feature which will be described in the next section). Thus my forecast for the likely start of a secular bear market in 2000 was consistent with a DG peak around this time. Since I considered the 1930's to be aberrant, I took my cues from the cycle before that. The DG peak in 1881-82 was accompanied by a burst of inflation. This seemed to have a parallel in late 1999 when the Federal Reserve was hiking rates to stave off inflation. Based on an analogy with the early 1880's, I believed that long rates would rise perhaps as high as 8% before coming down and I resolved to start buying bond funds in my taxable account (my 401K didn't have a bond fund option) when the 30 year treasury reached 7%. And I was to keep buying more at quarter point intervals until either the interest rate peak came or I ran out of cash, whichever came first. As I did not have a sound argument for this strategy, I did not write about it in *Stock Cycles*, which is a good thing, because it did not work; long rates never even got to 7%.

In my next book, *The Kondratiev Cycle*, I developed a transformation I called reduced price. Reduced price gives an indication of what prices would do in the absence of monetary stimulation. When applied to price data before

1933, reduced price shows the same Kondratiev up and down waves as do the unmodified prices. But when applied to data after 1933, it shows the K-cycle movements that lie "underneath" the raw price behavior that has been distorted by monetary simulation. I also learned of another tool, *ex-ante* real interest rates, which provides additional insight into monetary behavior over the K-cycle. These tools will be used to determine our current cycle position in the next section.

I also came up with the idea that the modern K-cycle was aligned with the Strauss and Howe saeculum, but with 18-year generations. A consequence of this work was that I now believed that the K-cycle was 72 years long—distinctly longer than 50-60 years. This meant that I now interpreted 2000 as the stock market "fall from plateau" (cycle-equivalent to 1929), and not the DG-peak (equivalent to 1937). It also meant that the Kondratiev trough, and end of the secular bear market, would likely come later, around 2018 and not 2010-14.

Another outcome from my work on *The Kondratiev Cycle* was the practice of using more than one cycle to interpret events and to make forecasts. I examined cycles of war and great power hegemony, social unrest, political ideology, and interwove them with the Kondratiev economic cycle and the Strauss and Howe generational cycle (saeculum). But in all this work there was still only one economic cycle that I was using, the Kondratiev. Hence, I undertook the study of other economic cycles presented in Chapter Two, which, hopefully, will provide additional insight into how this secular bear market will unfold over the next fifteen years or so. In the next section I will present the results of the reduced price and *ex-ante* interest rate analysis and relate them to the cycles introduced in Chapter Two.

Location in the K-cycle

Reduced prices are a normal price index, such as the PPI commodities index, divided by a theoretical price obtained from a simple monetary model:

4.1   Model Price = P_0 + V·S, where
$\qquad\qquad$ S = (money supply + cumulative federal deficit)/GDP

Here P_0 and V are parameters obtained by doing a linear regression of the actual price versus S over a moving 100 year period centered on the year of interest. S is what I call stimulation and is a measure of how much inflationary pressure is being applied by government deficit spending and by money expansion. The details of the calculation are given in Appendix C. Figure 4.1

shows a plot of reduced prices from 1790 to the present. Three full Kondratiev cycles and a portion of a fourth (the current one) are shown. Four Kondratiev peaks and troughs are shown. The spacing of these peaks and troughs average 55 years, in agreement with the typical 50-60 year length the K-cycle.

Figure 4.1. Reduced price and *ex-ante* real rate 1790-present

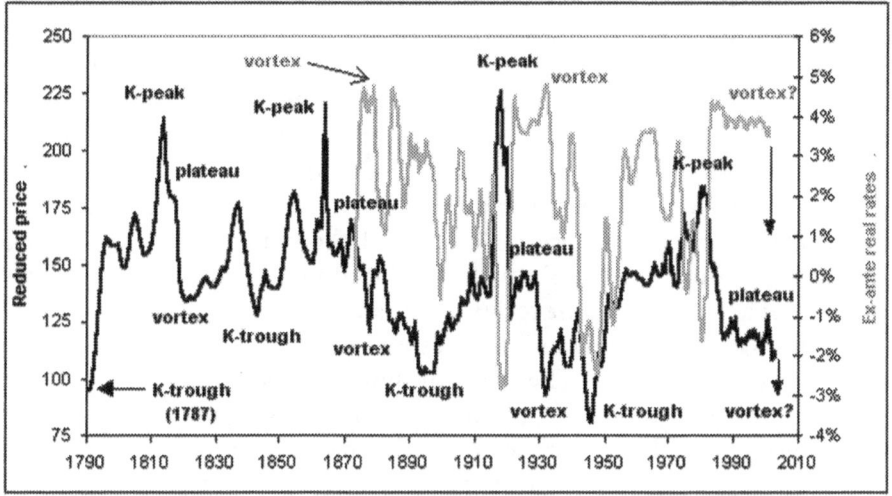

The period of rising prices between the Kondratiev trough and the Kondratiev peak is the Kondratiev upwave. Conversely, the decline from the peak to the trough is the downwave. Examination of the downwave in reduced prices shows a sharp drop after the Kondratiev peak and then a leveling-off. This level spot in the reduced price plot is sometimes called the *plateau*. The plateau ends with a second precipitous drop, the *fall from plateau*, which bottoms at the *vortex* (Berry, 1991). Figure 4.1 shows plateaus ending in 1818, 1872 and 1929, with a fourth possibly ending now. The vortices following the fall from plateau for the first three Kondratievs occurred in 1820, 1878 and 1932. Following the vortex, there is a temporary rise in prices to an intermediary peak, before prices fall still further to the Kondratiev trough. I call this intermediary the "deflationary growth peak" or DG-peak in accordance with Berry's (1991) nomenclature. DG-peaks occurred in 1836, 1881 and 1937 (a second larger peak in 1942 due to the start of WW II could be considered the DG peak instead of 1937; I prefer 1937 as it was more endogenously generated).

Also shown in Figure 4.1 is a new measure for the K-cycle, the *ex ante* real interest rate. The *ex ante* real rate is a measure of investors' collective beliefs about the future value of money. It cannot be measured directly, but it can be inferred from measurable data using complex mathematical models that are beyond my understanding. One such model, based on a regime switching framework (Hamilton, 1989) and implemented following Garcia and Perron's (1995) three-state interest rate model, has been recently proposed by Kolari and Viale (2001). This model shows investor beliefs about future real interest rates shifting between high-level (4-6%) and low-level (negative) regimes. Figure 4.1 shows a plot of the quarterly ex ante real rate obtained from Mr. Viale, which has been smoothed using a running nine-quarter moving average. The key feature of interest is the rise from a trough close to the K-peak to a broad plateau. This plateau ends right around the vortex in reduced prices, and then falls to a trough roughly around the time of the DG-peak. This trough is followed by another even deeper trough, which denotes the K-trough.

Examination of reduced price in Figure 4.1 shows the K-peak in 1981 and then a decline over 1981-86. Since 1986 reduced prices have been largely flat, suggestive of a plateau. *Ex-ante* real interest rate shows a major trough in 1980, corresponding to the K-peak and then a sharp rise over 1980-83. Since 1983 it has remained in a flat zone. The shape of these graphs shows what looks very much like a plateau period beginning in the mid-1980's. At the beginning of 2001, reduced prices began a major move downward that looked like it might be the start of the fall from plateau. Since the beginning of 2002 this fall has stalled out, however. As of October 2002, the PPI commodity index has been rising slightly faster than stimulation for the entire year. If the past pattern continues, *ex-ante* real rate should begin to fall again at some point in the near future and eventually reach a vortex bottom, which is still in the future.

So, although it looks very much like we are in the early stages of the fall from plateau, equivalent to 1930-1 in the last two cycles, this is not certain. The stock market peak in 2000 and spectacular bear market afterward are certainly consistent with this position, but the rising tendency of reduced prices through 2002 is not. A possible alternative is that the Dec 2001 bottom in reduced prices, the lowest since the downwave began in 1981, is the K-trough. This trough, occurring 55 years after the last K-trough in 1946, is consistent with the standard Kondratiev timing of 50-60 years.

This possibility would destroy the alignment between the Kondratiev cycle and the Strauss and Howe saeculum that is the centerpiece of my current thinking on cycles. But one has to consider the data. Although the saeculum provides an intriguing model to help explain why there should be cycles in the first place, it does not provide it s own independent milestones—there is no data to analyze. That is, there is no way to know the current position in the saeculum. Cycle turning points are apparent only in retrospect, which is hardly useful for forecasting purposes. So the saeculum cycle is of no direct help here. A Kondratiev trough today would also destroy the concept of Kondratiev seasons and their alignment with the Stock Cycle. This is more serious, as the Stock Cycle is based on real data that can be interpreted successfully in real time as I did in *Stock Cycles*. It is not likely that we are going to avoid a secular bear market. Such a bear market could unfold against the backdrop of a Kondratiev upwave, as it did for Great Britain over the 1897-1921 period. But this has not been the case for the US market. Because of the demonstrated success of the Stock Cycle, I do not place a great deal of confidence in the idea that the downwave is over.

The political cycle suggests a turning point around the time of the Stock Cycle/Kondratiev season/turning change. This shift should be from conservative to liberal. The GOP gains in the fall 2002 election suggest an endorsement of the conservative political principles of President Bush, suggesting a continuation of the conservative era that began some twenty years ago. The principles of the Bush administration seem to be similar to those of the Reagan administration. Both administrations vastly expanded deficit spending in order to fund military expansion. Both administrations proposed tax cuts on higher income house-holds as a means to stimulate the economy. There is a reasonable probability that pro-speculative economic policy will be continued. In saecular terms it would seem the unraveling is persisting. In Kondratiev terms this means that some of the unpleasant effects of Kondratiev winter may be delayed. If this interpretation is correct, the recent accounting mishaps will soon be forgotten and a new speculative bull market get underway.

The main point I wish to make is both of these alternate interpretations suggest a mildly inflationary future rather than a deflationary one. Both are bullish. The bearish deflationary scenario is inconsistent with the trend in reduced prices, the 2002 election results, the continued strength in real estate and consumer spending, the trend in unemployment (which hasn't risen sharply). Finally, there is my cycle analysis, which is cycle-consistent with the deflationist viewpoint (i.e. today is cycle-aligned with 1929-1932), but which is also bullish. So one does not have to buy my cycle analysis *in toto* to adopt a bullish stance to the stock market in fall 2002/spring 2003.

Where these viewpoints differ is in what happens later. The "K-trough is here" viewpoint holds that bonds will not be good long-term investments for the next 25 years. The continuation of the unraveling argument is similar to that of futurist Harry Dent (1998): stocks will rise well above their 2000 highs, but later in this decade they will peak and then bonds will be the preferred invest-ment as the economy heads into a depression. My view is bullish on stocks now, but will shift to bearish if and when the S&P500 moves to new all-time highs, at which point bonds are favored. For the rest of this chapter, I will make the assumption that my view on cycle location is correct, that we are at the fall from plateau and that there is a vortex in our future.

The meaning of our cycle location

Table 4.1 summarizes the Kondratiev cycle signposts using three criteria, stocks, reduced price, and the ex-ante real rate (ordinary interest rates for the first K-cycle and the 1861 K-peak). These signposts were derived from considerations of mostly monetary data: prices, money supply, interest rates, and stock prices. It is interesting to compare the dates to those obtained from the study of cycles in chapter two. The cycle dates in Chapter Two were obtained largely from consideration of a different set of data such as GDP, housing starts, real estate/land values, as well as stock prices. Looking at the first two Kondratievs in Table 4.1 it apparent that the plateau end reflects a Kuznets cycle peak with subsequent panic. The first three vortices reflect Kuznets troughs. The first two Kondratiev troughs are also Kuznet cycle troughs, and the DG-peak for the first Kondratiev is a Kuznets peak.

Table 4.1. Kondratiev markers in terms of three criteria

	Feature	K-peak	Plateau	Vortex	DG-peak	K-trough
Kondratiev I	Reduced Price	1814	1818	1821	1836	1842
(1787-1843)	Interest Rate	1814	–	1821	–	1830
	Stock	1815	1818	1819	1835	1843
Kondratiev II	Reduced Price	1864	1872	1878	1881	1897
(1843-1897)	Ex-ante interest rate	1861[1]	–	1878	1882	1899
	Stock	1861	1872	1877	1881	1896
Kondratiev III	Reduced Price	1918	1929	1932	1937	1946
(1897-1949)	Ex ante interest rate	1920	–	1932	1937	1946
	Stock	1921	1929	1932	1937	1949
Kondratiev IV	Reduced Price	1981	2001	future	future	future
(1949-present)	Ex ante interest rate	1980	–	future	future	future
	Stock	1982	2000	2002?	future	future

[1]   based on ordinary interest rates

It appears that the features I have identified as Kondratiev milestones, implying that they were produced by the K-cycle, were actually largely generated by the Kuznets cycle in the early Kondratievs. That is, to a certain extent, the structure of the early Kondratiev cycle is an artifact caused by the interaction of the Kuznets real-estate cycle with the Kondratiev monetary cycle. What this means is that evidence from these early cycles may not be relevant today. For example, in *Stock Cycles* I noted that secular market trends last from 7 to 20 years. The 7 year period comes from the 1835-42 secular bear market, which followed a very long 20-year secular bull market. But if the start of this secular bear market simply reflected the Kuznets cycle, the long 1815-35 secular bull market and short 1835-42 secular bear market may simply be an artifact with little relevance for the modern economy.

However, the 1881-2 DG peak is *not* Kuznets-related. It reflects the roaring economic boom and powerful bull market than emerged from the 1877-78 vortex. This boom was related to the expansion of the railroads and the industrial economy that went along with it, which I had called "the railroad/industrial economy" in *Stock Cycles*. The periodic appearance of a new economy is a Kondratiev feature and so some aspects of the structure shown in Table 4.1 are Kondratiev in nature. Thus, the 1872 Kuznets peak did *not* end the 1861-81 secular bull market, showing a growing importance of the Kondratiev cycle in the stock market and economy.

As discussed in Chapter Two, the Kuznets cycle declined in power while the Kondratiev cycle gained in the early part of the 20th century until after 1933 the former no longer exerted much of an effect on long economic cycles. Thus, although the fall from plateau in 1929-32 did follow the 1925 Kuznets peak, it did so with a noticeable lag. The bulk of the 1920's secular bull market occurred after the 1925 Kuznets peak, and it is more likely that the peak in stock valuation triggered the Depression than the peak in land values. Finally, the 1946/49 Kondratiev and Stock Cycle troughs were not close to a Kuznets trough. Similarly, stocks collapsed in 2000, producing a powerful bear market than is almost certainly the start of a secular bear market, (and possibly the fall from plateau) while the Kuznets cycle continues to rise. So there are important Kondratiev features that exist independently of the Kuznets cycle that seem to be relevant today.

These features are linked to the cycle of "new economies" that Harry Dent calls the innovation wave and which were discussed at length in my previous books. The current "information economy" is still in what Harry Dent (1993) calls the Growth Boom, which began around 1981 and is not supposed to end until sometime around 2007. A continuation of the 1990's growth in the new economy is to be expected. The innovation wave argues that instead of a 2000's decade of really poor growth, as many bearish commentators suggest, more of the same kind of investment-led growth is yet in store. Of course right now, the business investment activity is dismal, reflecting massive over-investment in the late 1990's. One might expect a new boom in business investment to begin toward the middle of the current Juglar cycle, or around 2004-6. In the meantime, consumer demand should remain strong, powered by the still rising Kuznets cycle.

Just about the time that business investment begins to really get going as the Juglar cycle moves into its boom phase, the Kuznets cycle will peak and begin to exert a drag on the economy. Thus, a repeat of the exuberant late nineties in the stock market is not likely. The next recession, expected to occur near the end of this decade, should bring in the Kuznets bottom.

When the vortex will develop is unclear. If such a feature is even still present, it should show up as a trough in reduced price. Examination of the post-1933 behavior of reduced prices in Figure 4.1 shows only two periods during which a significant decline in reduced price occurred. The first time was the 1937-46 period, which showed a decline reflecting actual deflation from 1937 to 1940, followed by a spike up to 1942 reflecting the start of WW II, and then a sharp drop to the trough in 1946. This second drop did not reflect deflation, but rather a slower rate of inflation that what was called for by the massive increase in stimulation (S) caused by WW II deficit spending. The second time was the decline from 1981 to 1986, which also did not reflect any real deflation, but rather, slower inflation than what was called for by the rapid rise in S caused by substantial deficit spending.

The general theme of these declines is that a drop in reduced price is caused more by a rise in S than a drop in actual price. The decline in reduced price in 2001 reflected both a drop in actual prices and a rise in S. The sizable deficit now developing suggests a strongly rising S in the future, but since the beginning of 2002 price rises have kept pace with rising S, preventing reduced price from falling further. Should a decline start up again in the near future a trough identifiable as a vortex could appear in a few years. If this happens the vortex would be coincident with a Kuznets peak instead of a trough as it has in past cycles. But all past vortices have been in the pre-regulated era, so their prior example may no longer be relevant.

Both of the declines in reduced prices considered above ended at or near bull market peaks; the 1946 trough was a bull market peak, and the December 1986 end of the post-1981 decline was less than one year before the 1987 bull market peak. Based on the five-year drop from 1981 to 1986, it is likely that any fall from plateau beginning in 2001 would take a long time, possibly to 2008. This is the nominal date for the Kitchin cycle peak (and likely bull market top) immediately preceding the next Juglar and Kuznets bottom in ~2010. What this suggests is reduced prices could show a gradual drop to a significant bottom at the same time as stocks advance over the next 5 or 6 years.

If past patterns are still valid, the vortex should show the beginning of a significant decline in *ex-ante* real interest rates. This drop in *ex-ante* real rates signals a shift in monetary regime. Prior to the shift (when *ex-ante* rates are still in the high regime) the bond market serves as a gauge of future inflation. A current inflation rate of 2 or 3% should result in long term government bond rates of 5 or 6% with neutral inflation expectations. Interest rates would be higher if inflation is expected to rise and lower if it is expected to fall. Recent lows below 5% on the 30-year bond suggest inflation expectations of less than 2%, which are consistent with actual observed inflation, suggesting that we remain in the high rate regime.

The regime change involves a shift in how the bond market prices government bonds. Pricing ceases to be based on inflationary expectations. After the regime shift long-term government rates could easily fall below the inflation rate, as happened in the 1930's, 1940's and 1970's. Recently, Federal Reserve Governor Benjamin Bernanke (2002) gave a speech that puts the idea of a regime change into policy terms:

> Historical experience tends to support the proposition that a sufficiently determined Fed can peg or cap Treasury bond prices and yields at other than the shortest maturities. The most striking episode of bond-price pegging occurred during the years before the Federal Reserve-Treasury Accord of 1951. Prior to that agreement, which freed the Fed from its responsibility to fix yields on government debt, the Fed maintained a ceiling of 2-1/2 percent on long-term Treasury bonds for nearly a decade. Moreover, it simultaneously established a ceiling on the twelve-month Treasury certificate of between 7/8 percent to 1-1/4 percent and, during the first half of that period, a rate of 3/8 percent on the 90-day Treasury bill. The Fed was able to achieve these low interest rates despite a level of outstanding government debt (relative to GDP) significantly greater than we have today, as well as inflation rates substantially more variable. At times, in order to enforce these low rates, the Fed had actually to purchase the bulk of outstanding 90-day bills. Interestingly, though, the Fed enforced the 2-1/2 percent ceiling on long-term bond yields for nearly a decade without ever holding a substantial share of long-maturity bonds outstanding. For example, the Fed held 7.0 percent of outstanding Treasury securities in 1945 and 9.2 percent in 1951 (the year of the Accord), almost entirely in the form of 90-day bills. For comparison, in 2001 the Fed held 9.7 percent of the stock of outstanding Treasury debt.

The Fed actions to which Bernanke is referring are actions the Federal Reserve might employ to fight deflation. Basically they involve massive injection of money into the economy, by manipulation of interest rates other than just the Federal Funds rate, the normal tool of policy. This would boost S and drive reduced prices down towards a vortex. Simultaneously, they would also serve to break the relation between long-term interest rates and inflation; that is, they would produce the regime change in *ex-ante* interest rates.

If the past behavior is still relevant, such actions should occur around the time of the vortex. Unless the shallow drop in reduced prices in 2001 was all that will happen, the vortex is still to come and these actions will not be necessary today. Indeed, the bullish arguments made in the last two chapters suggest that recovery will occur without further intervention. However, things are likely to be less bullish for the next recession. Also, it is not likely that a great deal of tightening will be achieved in the next expansion, meaning that when the next recession hits, Fed manipulations that will lead to the regime shift will probably have to be implemented.

What this means is government long bonds are not recommended now, stocks should do better. As the stock market approaches its 2000 highs (in constant dollars), stocks should be sold on a scale and long-term government bonds bought. The regime shift will likely mean very low interest rates on long bonds in the next recession, which should produce a once-in-a-lifetime bonanza for those buying bonds near the end of this expansion. Although valuations will have improved significantly; stocks will likely not perform as well in the 2010's as they will in this decade and bonds will be particularly bad investments after the regime shift.

The above analysis assumes that a vortex will indeed develop and that the regime shift will happen then, as was the case in the last two cycles. But this reflects what happened before 1933; it could be different now. There is little risk, however. No decision to invest in bonds need be made until well after a new bull market in stocks gets underway, which hasn't even happened yet. Long before a sell level is reached it will be clear whether reduced price has continued its 2001 decline to much lower levels or not. If not, then there will be no vortex in the old sense of the word and no reason to believe that something like a regime shift is going to happen. In this case, government bonds are not particularly favored as an alternative to stocks. If reduced prices actually head strongly upwards over the next few years, this suggests that the deflationary character of the downwave may be over (either a new upwave has started or that the 2001 low was the vortex). Bonds are not recommended in this case.

Outlook for gold

In this section I use the concepts presented above to chart a course for the long-term (10-20 years) path for gold prices. Gold is a unique asset in that is both a commodity and a monetary instrument. As a metal, it is subject to the same sorts of supply and demand pressures that apply to other metallic commodities. Gold has commercial uses and has a production cost, just like other commodities. Unlike other commodities, however, gold has often served as money in the past and thus has a use as a store of value (i.e. savings). That is, gold may be accumulated (hoarded) for the purposes of saving in a way that other commodities are not. For example, central banks and private investors hold large stocks of the metal relative to annual production and consumption. The willingness of gold owners to keep large stocks of the metal out of economic use means that gold can trade (for years) way out of line with the supply and demand strictures that apply to other commodities. The reason gold is accumulated is that it has served as money in the past and still retains an association with money for a considerable fraction of the world's population.

What this means is the concept of monetary stimulation (S) and reduced prices should have special relevance for gold, even today. Back in the late 19th and early 20th centuries, the American dollar was on the gold standard. What this means is the U.S. dollar was set as equal in value to a fixed quantity (about 1/21 of a troy ounce) of pure gold. This peg to gold produced financial manipulations which resulted in the money supply of the U.S. growing no faster than economic activity. It also discouraged government deficit spending, except during times of war, when the government would go off the gold standard. Expressed in terms of the reduced price concept, the gold standard kept monetary stimulation (S) at a roughly constant value. Except during times of war, S remained in a range, and so reduced prices closely tracked regular prices. As a result, the Kondratiev cycle, which is manifested as a cycle in reduced prices, also showed up in regular prices as well. During Kondratiev downwaves, prices would fall, causing considerable economic hardship. This hardship produced calls for "free silver" in the late 19th century downwave and brought in modern Keynesian economic management in the downwave after that. Today this same concern has produced "Greenspanism".

Figure 4.2 outlines the history of gold prices and how the various efforts to deal with pernicious downwaves have changed the course of gold prices. The "money" role of gold means that one should be able to apply the stimulation concept used to produce reduced prices to the price of gold. Figure 4.2 shows a stimulation-based model for the price of gold. This model simply assumes that gold price is proportional to the stimulation model for ordinary prices that is used to calculate the reduced price. For the period 1860-1915, the market price of gold (POG) and the stimulation model closely agree. The only discrepancy is in the 1862-1879 period. In order to finance the Civil War, the U.S. government had to resort to a fiat currency in the form of Greenbacks. Doing so took the U.S. financial system "off gold" in 1862. It was only in 1879 that the dollar came back to "parity" with gold and the U.S. went back on the gold standard (Roper and Warner, 1991). What this means is the price for gold given by the stimulation model (the true value of gold as "money") rose above the POG in 1862 and didn't fall back until 1879.

Figure 4.2. Annotated price history of gold

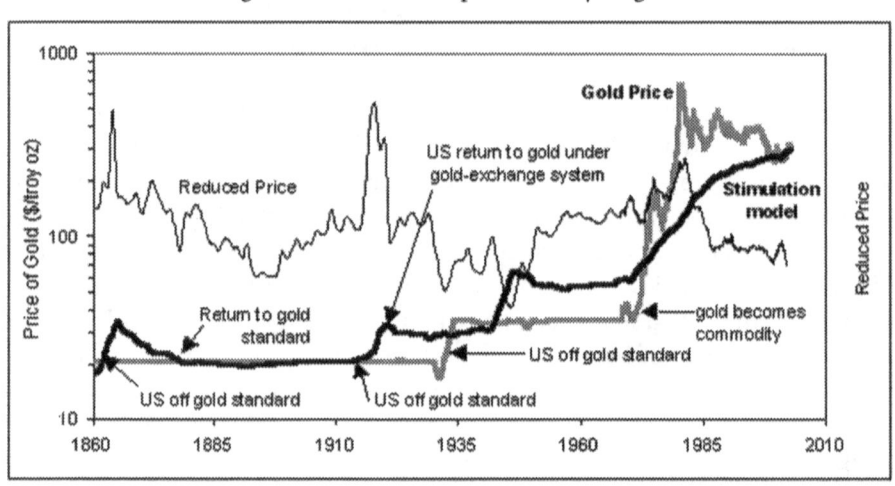

From 1879 to just before World War I, the U.S. dollar was on the gold standard. This is shown in Figure 4.2 by the close correspondence between the price of gold predicted by the stimulation model and the POG. This is necessary because the whole purpose of a gold standard is to regulate stimulation in such a way that this correspondence occurs. During WW I, the U.S. (and the rest of the WW I belligerents) went off the gold standard just as the U.S. had done for the Civil War. After the war, the U.S. (and eventually the rest of the Western world) went back onto gold. But this return to gold was *not* at parity (Roper and Girton, 1993). That is, the POG was well below what the stimulation model calls for. For parity to be reached would require politically unacceptable levels of deflation after World War I and so the gold standard was re-established under what was called the gold-exchange system (Roper and Girton, 1993). Throughout the 1920's, the economic authorities were able to maintain stable currencies well above the value consistent with gold. When the world economy "fell off the plateau" after the 1929 stock crash, the gold exchange system was no longer tenable and one country after another went off gold. The U.S. left gold in 1933 and a new POG was established at $35 an ounce by a devaluation of the dollar.

World War II introduced another round of stimulation. As a result, the price of gold given by the stimulation model once again rose above the POG. This time the world did not return to the gold standard. Instead, the world currencies were pegged to the U.S. dollar, which was then pegged to gold at $35 per ounce. The strong trade position of the U.S. coupled with the vast gold reserves of the U.S. treasury meant that the U.S. could keep this new "dollar system" going for decades despite the lack of parity between the dollar and gold. Eventually the system collapsed in 1971 and gold began to trade as a commodity. After more than two decades of under-valuation, the POG exploded upward after 1971. Now freed of its monetary characteristics, gold began to behave as a commodity. As the world economy progressed through the inflationary Kondratiev summer period, gold rose in price along with oil and other commodities reaching a peak around the time of the K-peak in 1980-81. Gold rose partly as a response to its previous under-valuation, and partly as a commodity following the K-cycle as defined in reduced prices (see Figure 4.2).

By 1980, gold had become extremely overvalued relative to its value as money. The very fact that gold has been used historically as money suggests that it has a higher value as money than any other use, implying that gold was extremely overvalued relative to any use. Thus, once the Kondratiev downwave got underway after 1981 gold would be expected to fall dramatically in price, which is exactly what it did (Figure 4.2). In recent years, gold has reached parity with the dollar again. That is, gold is no longer either over or undervalued compared to the dollar. Now this does not mean that gold cannot move lower from here. Recall the lengthy periods in the 1920's and the 1940's through 1960's during which the POG was well below its monetarily-derived value. The economic authorities have in the past held the POG well below its money value for decades. Also the deflationary drag of the fall from plateau should exert a negative pull on the POG in is role as a commodity. On the other hand, gold's role as a store of value could benefit from the uncertainty that accompanies the fall from plateau. Hence the POG should fluctuate as these two forces attempt to push it in one direction or another.

What will likely happen during the fall from plateau is a substantial rise in stimulation. During the 1981-87 fall to plateau the stimulation-based price of gold (bold black line in Figure 4.2) rose from about $135 to $210. The POG was much higher than this, however, and so it fell during this time. If the current fall from plateau is accompanied by a similar degree of stimulation, the stimulation-based price of gold would rise from $285 to $440. This suggests that gold purchased at recent lows (260's-280's) should eventually be a good long-term investment (it has already proven to be a good short-term investment). Note that just because the stimulation model for gold is rising does *not* mean that the POG must rise at the same time. Figure 4.2 contains abundant evidence that this is not true. What it *does* mean is if the POG falls back again, gold (or gold mining stocks) purchased at those lower levels will be undervalued for the first time since 1973.

Right now (Nov 2002) with the stimulation model showing $300 and POG around $310-20, gold is not undervalued nor particularly overvalued. There is no monetary driver for gold to move higher or lower and so gold should respond to the same sorts of price pressures facing commodities, and to psychological factors. The fall off plateau exerts a deflationary effect on the economy, which although countered by massive stimulation, has kept inflation low. Short term rates are very low, while long-term rates are still fairly high. Based on the stimulation model for gold, it would seem that recent lows in the $260-280's range should fall into the lower region of gold's trading range over the next 10-20 years. The unsettled nature of markets at this time suggests that opportunities to accumulate at these levels or even lower could well appear in the next few years. The long-term trend in the stimulation model suggests that such accumulations will outperform money markets in the longer run.

Chapter 5

Asset Allocation in my 401(k)

In this chapter, I describe what I actually did in my 401K since I completely left stocks on September 3, 1999. In principle, it seems straightforward enough. During a secular bull market trend long term investors such as myself should be fully invested in stocks. Once a secular bear market trend has begun, asset allocation between stock and non-stock investments should be guided by valuation concerns.

Once there is reason to believe that a secular bear market has begun, asset allocation strategy changes from fully invested in stocks to a mixture of stocks and non-stock investments. The stock index can still outperform money markets if they are purchased at "low enough" prices, or if purchased at short-term low prices and sold after a relatively short period of time. How to change asset allocation as the secular bear market progresses will depend on two things, market valuation and investor risk tolerance. For investors with low risk tolerance and a 5+ year time horizon, the "safe" level is given by equation 5.1:

5.1.   safe level $= 500 \, (1.02 + i/100)^N$

Here i is the average inflation rate in the future and N is the number of years after 2001. The safe level refers to the level of the S&P500 below which long-term investments in this index will almost certainly outperform money markets if held for 5 years or more. The levels given by Equation 5.1 are so low they are not likely to be reached anytime in the near future. The purpose of this equation is to keep risk-adverse investors entirely out of the market during the secular bear market, only reentering when it is nearing its end (or a stupendous buying opportunity like summer 1932 emerges). More enterprising investors will want to avail themselves of the potential gains to be had during secular bear markets, keeping the risk in mind, of course.

My view in early 2001

In *Stock Cycles* the key valuation parameter employed was *relative* P/R (rPR). This is the value of P/R divided by its average value during the preceding Stock

Cycle. For the current period, rPR is P/R divided by its average value over the previous 34 years. I used this tool in Stock Cycles to estimate the value of the S&P500 index relative to its long-term (30 years) future performance. I also used it to make the forecast that stocks won't beat money markets over the next twenty years. Relative P/R reached an all-time high of 2.29 in July 1999, based on the monthly average of the index. In March and August of the next year, relative P/R reached the same peak level, before beginning a dramatic drop.

The Peaks in rPR tend to occur near the end of the secular bull markets, sometimes right at the top such as in June 1881 or September 1929. Other times they precede the top, sometimes by a considerable amount of time. For example, rPR peaked in December 1961, four years before the secular bull top in January 1966. The June 1901 rPR peak preceded the September 1906 top by more than five years. Finally the first rPR peak in July 1999 had so far preceded the apparent March 2000 bull market top by eight months. Another bull rally that would have carried the index to a marginal new constant-dollar high in another year or so could not be ruled out in early 2001. Had this happened, it would have made the official end of the secular bull market later than March 2000.

Shorter-term investments late in a secular bull market can be profitable because of the uncertainly that a secular bear market has in fact begun. Until a new bull market fails to exceed the previous bull market peak, some investors will believe that the secular bull market is still in progress. Bullish models, such as Harry Dent's (1998), will also provide support for the bullish thesis. As a result, investors would be much more aggressive with long positions in early 2001 than they would be years later.

I wished to take advantage of this situation. In my company's 401K program employees have a choice of several stock funds, an income fund, and a blended stock/bond fund. There was no pure bond fund then (this has changed since then). One of the stock funds is an S&P500 index fund. The funds I used for my allocation were American Century Ultra (TWCUX) and the income fund. Ultra shows a higher degree of volatility than the index fund and so is more suitable for the asset allocation scheme I had in mind. The income fund is like a money market fund in that it does not decline in value, but it is invested primarily in asset-backed securities and tends to give a return that follows longer-term interest rates. Over the 1999-2001 period it yielded about 6%.

Figure 5.1. American Century Ultra (TWCUX) and buying/selling points.

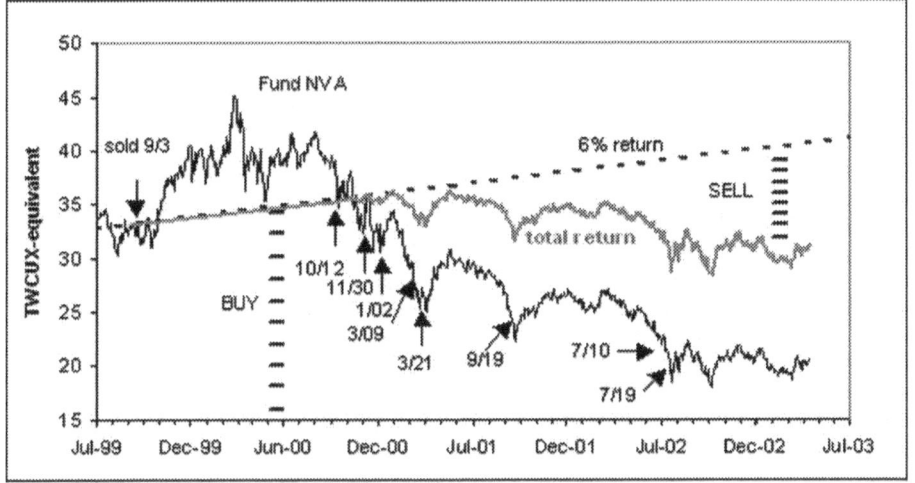

Figure 5.1 shows a graph of American Century Ultra with arrows marking my final sale on September 3, 1999 and subsequent repurchases of TWCUX. After I moved completely out of TWCUX in September 1999, my 401K was earning a 6% return, while TWCUX advanced 35% to its peak in March 2000. As a long-term investor, I should not concern myself with short-term movements like this, but it was difficult to sit on the sidelines and watch the market do things I never thought it could do (such the NASDAQ soaring to 5000+). During the NASDAQ minicrash from March to May 2000, I saw evidence that perhaps I would again be able to buy TWCUX at prices below where I had exited. That May, I decided I would begin to buy on a wide scale as soon at TWCUX dropped decisively below my exit level (adjusted for the return I had gotten since then in the income fund).

Having decided where to start re-entry into the market, I needed to ascertain where the bottom of my scale buying would be. That is, how low would the market have to go for me to be 100% invested in stocks? In Chapter 4 of *Stock Cycles*, I presented a model I developed that described the behavior of the market over shorter periods of time. This model suggested that as long as earnings growth continued unabated (that is, we would have no recession) the stock market would continue climbing. The very optimistic forecasts of Dow 36,000 and higher made by various bullish analysts would actually come true if the ten-year old expansion keep right on going for another 7-10 years. If it came to an end there would instead by a rather severe bear market, which would very likely mark the beginning of a secular bear market predicted by P/R.

In *Stock Cycles*, I used the model to analyze a hypothetical recession that started with an earnings peak at the end of 1999. The model I developed is not predictive—one of the inputs into the model is the index value—so to use the model one must know what the market will do. Of course one doesn't know the future path the market will take. What one *can* do is put in various hypothetical market scenarios into the model and see if they are consistent with past behavior. So I inputted a hypothetical recession by using the last recession as a template. By doing this I found that at a recession market bottom the S&P500 would have to be in a range of 650 to 1360 for it to be consistent with past behavior. So the worst case for a recession beginning at an earnings peak at the end of 1999 would be about 650 on the S&P500-assuming a recession of 1990 severity. Since earnings did not peak at the end of 1999, they would necessarily peak higher and so I picked 700 as a bottom. Looking back to when the S&P500 had been around 700 I found that TWCUX was in the 16-17 range at that time. So I determined that I would buy on a wide scale starting a bit under 35 and going all the way down to 16.5, if necessary (see buy bars in Figure 5.1). I also developed a set of sell rules (see Figure 5.1) which were never used and which are now irrelevant.

Having defined both the buying and selling scales the operation now became quite mechanical. On October 12, 2000 the market dipped strongly and I moved 10% of my 401K from income to TWCUX at a net asset value of 34.61. By March 21, 2001 I reached a 50% invested level with TWCUX at 25.71. This was the situation when I wrote my first asset-allocation article in May 2001 (Alexander, 2001) in order to provide a real-time record of how this strategy had fared. If TWCUX continued to fall I would continue to increase my stock allocation in accordance with the BUY lines. If TWCUX rose above 35, I would sell in accordance with the SELL lines.

The market did continue to fall in the months after May 2001 and I bought again, on September 19 2001. TWCUX was low enough to buy yet again on September 21, 2001 but as it is a fund, I wasn't sure of what its price was going to be that day. Besides, I figured (after I missed the buy and saw that it was "low enough") that I could buy the next day or next week on the retest (as it was almost certainly going lower). That was as low as she went that time. By the time I wrote my second asset allocation article seven months later in April 2002 (Alexander 2002b), it still hadn't gone lower. Nevertheless I continued to hold 40% in the income fund against the possibility that it might. It was completely possible that in the coming months we would go still lower than the Sept 21 lows and my allocation in TWCUX would increase, but at that point it was at 60%.

Now one might ask, if I had stayed completely invested in the income fund until Sept 19, 2001, I could have moved 60% to TWCUX at that price instead of the much higher price at which I owned it. The net result would be the same as where I actually was in spring 2002, except I would be ahead some 6-7%. The reason why I didn't do this was because I didn't *know* it would get to the September 19 levels in the first place. And when it finally did reach that level, was that a good buy? How would I know that it wasn't going any lower? There was no more reason in September 2001 (when I was 60% invested) to believe that the market was going to go up than there was in April 2001 (50% invested) or in January 2001 (30% invested), or indeed in October 2000 (10% invested). There is never clear evidence when such a movement is going to happen. If there were, we could all be rich.

As it turned out, September 21, 2001 was no more the bottom than were April 4, 2001, January 2, 2001 or October 12, 2000. On July 10, 2002 I bought again, bringing my stock allocation up to 70% (Alexander 2002c). This time there was a twist. My company dropped TWCUX as a 401K investment option in June 2002 and I was forced to move my assets from TWCUX to an index fund. The specific fund is an institutional S&P500 index fund that has no symbol, so I will use the Vanguard index fund (VFINX) as a proxy. The Fund NVA line in Figure 5.2 is a graph of the American Century Ultra fund up to September 19, 2001 and VFINX after this date (VFINX is scaled so that it dovetails with TWCUX on 9/19/01). The new buy on July 10 reflects the fact that VFINX was substantially lower on that date than it was in September, low enough to have reached another buy line. A week later I bought again, on July 19, 2002 (Alexander 2002d). I missed the October 9, 2002 bottom. It just *barely* qualified as another purchase, and rose so quickly afterward that no other date has qualified so far (March 2003). However, so far none of the other bottoms have held and I will not be surprised if I am buying again at yet lower lows in the future. I retain the 20% income position against that possibility.

Also shown in Figure 5.1 is a gray line, which shows total return in my 401K since Sept 3, 1999. The presentation in Figure 5.1 suggests that any reliance on stocks for my 401K is foolish. That is, I would have been better off staying fully invested in the safe income fund, as I was before 1995. In actuality this was not true, TWCUX handily outperformed the income fund over the 1995-2000 period. Figure 5.2 presents the total return obtained by the actual mix of stock and income funds in my 401K after 10/23/97 (when I started keeping a record of my 401K allocations). Also shown are the returns from a 100% position in stocks (TWCUX until 9/19/02, VFINX after) and a 100% position in the income fund (assumed to be a fixed 6% return over the entire period).

Having stocks contributed strongly to total return during the bull market. From 10/23/97 to the bull market peak on 3/24/00, my 401K mix advanced 43% compared to 99% for TWCUX, and only 15% for the income fund. At this time it appeared that the mix strategy in my 401K, although far better than the straight income strategy I used before 1995, was doomed to underperform the stock market. At the end of March 2003, the total return from 10/23/97 of my 401K mix strategy has been 31% compared to a 14% *loss* for the all-stock strategy and 37% gain for the all-income strategy.

So *both* stocks and the safe investment options have a role to play in maximization of returns. The stock accumulation begun in October 2000 has substantially depressed my returns over what I would have gotten had I maintained a 100% income stance. Yet if I had done so, I must also consider the negative effect of holding the income fund instead of the stock fund during bull market periods. I should note that the *entire* period covered by Figure 5.2 has been a time of record stock market P/E and a 100% income stance in the late 1990's would have been in order (and is *still* in order) were I following Shiller's P/E or Tobin's Q.

Figure 5.2. Overall 401K return since 10/23/97 compared to stock and fixed 6% return

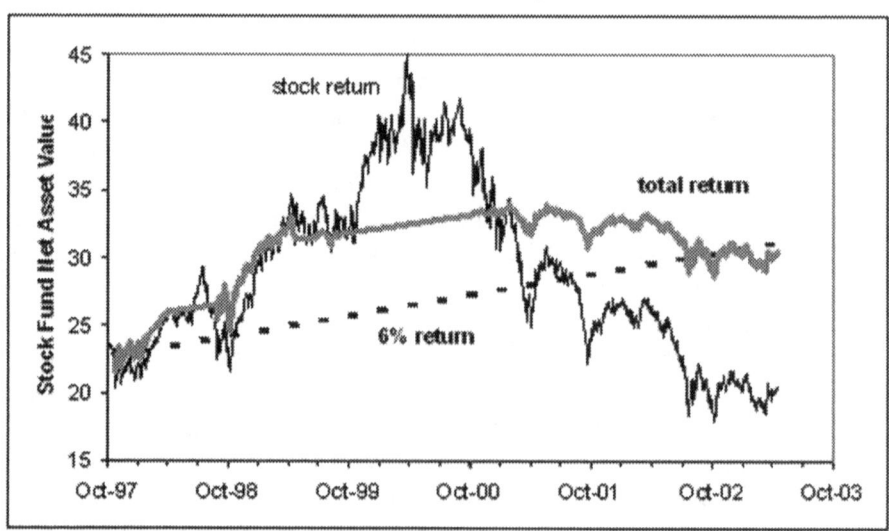

One can point out that if the S&P500 were to fall further from its present value the total return of the mix strategy from 1997 would fall even further behind that from the income fund. This is completely true, and as the market falls the stock allocation will increase, accelerating the erosion of total return. Should the S&P500 fall to ~700, at which point my method calls for 100% stock allocation, total return from Oct 1997 would be 21%, substantially behind the income return. In this case, the blend strategy will look decidedly inferior to the all-income strategy, just as the blend strategy looked inferior compared to the all-stock strategy in March 2000. But should that visit to 700 be followed by a strong bull market, the 100% stock allocation that would be in place would get the full benefit of that bull advance, likely putting the blend strategy substantially ahead of the income strategy once again.

But one can point out that by staying in the income fund until 700 is reached and then buying, a much better return will be obtained. This is true of course, but if one has stayed in income from October 1997 though the 1997-2000 bubble and then through the 50% collapse that followed the bubble, would one have the courage to go long? Consider that both Shiller's P/E and Tobin's Q indicate that the market has *much* further to fall at an S&P500 of 700. After all, if we use the 1929-32 bear market as a model, a 50% decline in the S&P500 could be followed by *another* 50% decline and the level reached would *still* be some 70% *higher* than the 1932 bottom. In other words, just as a bull market can always go higher (in the short term), a bear market can always go lower. Also, the S&P500 has not yet gone as low as 700, and might not. In this case, an investor waiting for this level to be reached in order to buy would remain out of stocks for the eventual bull market.

In the real world, when faced with a powerful bear, many investors will wait until it is clear that the bear has gone before re-entering the market. And usually that means the bull market has to have recovered 50% or more of the bear market decline before it starts to look like a bull market and not just another bear market rally. Should a new bull market have begun on October 9, 2002, will investors who fled the markets get back in early enough to benefit? Only time will tell.

Discussion and evaluation

In retrospect, it is clear that I re-entered the market too soon. I began purchasing when the market was still extremely high. Part of the reason I was willing to buy so early was what I was buying. The American Century Ultra fund was already down more than 20% from its high at my first purchase, because of its heavy NASDAQ component. I would not have started buying the S&P500 index fund at that early juncture.

Another reason was I was focused on *relative* P/R valuation, which gave a fairly optimistic picture of potential gains. Relative P/R had peaked years before the ultimate secular bull market peak in two of the three most recent secular bear markets. I wasn't expecting that the first decline in this secular bear market would be particularly large. My thinking was more along the lines of the 1962 or 1966 bear markets, not something along the lines of the 1973-74 megabear. There was good reason for such thinking. The previous secular bear market had reached high levels only in terms of rPR—absolute P/R was the lowest of any secular bull market peak. Even the 1929 peak wasn't particularly high in P/R terms, only in terms of rPR was it extremely high. In fact, I had developed relative P/R to deal with this very fact. The two worst secular bear markets had been preceded by a market peak that was not particularly high in terms of P/R, but was very high in terms of relative rPR. Hence I gave a lot of credence to this measure. Even as late as spring 2002, I was still of the opinion the percentage drop in P/R from its 2000 peak would be more comparable to past experience than the absolute value of P/R. That is, I was still thinking in *relative* terms.

But as the figures in Chapter 3 show, the market fell until absolute P/R reached levels consistent with past secular bear markets. Hence in this book I have focused on P/R valuation and not rPR, which featured prominently in Stock Cycles. What I did right was stick to my scale all the way down. I did not, for example, add an extra allocation of stocks in late November 2001 when it appeared that the worst was over and a new bull market was underway. I stuck to my strategy of only buying should the market fall below its September 2001 levels to my next buy level. And so when it did in summer 2002 I still had plenty of buying power to add stock at lower levels. And as of this writing (March 2003) I still have 20% of my 401K assets uncommitted, ready to be deployed should the market go still lower.

As long as the ultimate low is within the range of my scale buying, I will be assured of getting at least one position fairly close to the bottom. This position, and the few next-higher ones, will produce the bulk of the gains in the subsequent rally. If the strategy proves to be successful these final few positions will produce sufficient gains for my whole 401K portfolio to have out-performed the safe alternative over in the post-1999 era.

Chapter 6

Putting It Together,
Plotting a Strategy

The basic message given in *Stock Cycles* was that stocks outperform other investments during secular bull markets and that long-term investors should be fully invested in stocks during these periods. With the end of the secular bull market in 2000, the task of investing becomes much more difficult. When I first discovered what I would eventually call P/R valuation in 1995, I knew that at some time I would have to figure out some sort of investment strategy to employ once the secular bull market ended. By extrapolating the 1982-1995 rise forward and estimating future P/R values, I projected that the end was still comfortably far off in the future. I simply transferred 100% of my 401K from the income fund to a stock fund in September 1995 and let it ride.

There were two basic ways to deal with the coming secular bear market. One would be to exploit the shorter-term trends by learning market timing. Another way would be to pick stocks that will do well despite the secular bear market and invest in those. I decided to try my hand at market timing by switching funds back and forth between the income fund and the stock fund in my 401K. First I read up on technical analysis. I was not interested in being a very active trader; my goal was to trade the secondary trends (the multi-month rallies and corrections). I wasn't very good at it.

I also read up on fundamental analysis, especially value-style investing, and tried my hand at this in my taxable account over 1997-99. I was even worse at stock picking. I finally fell back on a dynamic asset allocation strategy based on an idea I got from a book called *How to Make $1,000,000 in the Stock Market Automatically* by Robert Lichello (1977). Lichello's method starts with a 50% stock, 50% cash portfolio. The stock allocation is increased if the portfolio falls below a deadband value and decreases if the portfolio rises above. My strategy was described in the previous chapter. In the next section a superior timing strategy is presented that is based on the four year Kitchen cycle described in chapter two.

Market timing using the four-year cycle

One outcome from the cycle work in Chapter Two is a possible timing strategy that exploits the Kitchin cycle in the stock market. It has been suggested that a good strategy would be to buy stocks in the fall of non-presidential election years, and sell at the end of presidential election years (HR Consultants, 1997). To test this idea I calculated total returns for index purchases made at the average index closing price in September of non-presidential election years and sales made at the average index close in December of presidential election years.

Before 1933 the strategy was distinctly inferior to merely holding the stock index continuously. But this is not surprising since the four year cycle only emerged after 1933. For the period starting in Dec 1936 and ending in September 2002, a fully invested stance would have returned 10.0% annually, whereas use of the four year cycle would have given slightly better results at 10.8%. It is interesting to see how these two strategies fared during the secular bull and bear periods (Table 6.1).

The four-year strategy handily beat the always-invested strategy during the secular bear markets, most noticeably in the current secular bear market. But it lost relative to the always-invested strategy during the secular bull markets, giving up most of the relative gains made during the bear period. This observation suggests, why not apply the four year timing cycle only during the secular bear market periods? This approach gives superior results during the secular bear markets, yet preserves most of the gains during secular bull markets. Obviously, I did not know about this strategy in 1999 or I would have employed it.

Table 6.1 Results of different timing strategies during secular bull and bear markets

Period	Always invested	Invested during Sec bulls only	4-year cycle	4-year cycle sec bears only
1937-1949	3.2%	0.27%	4.4%	4.4%
1949-1966	16.7%	16.7%	11.0%	13.8%
1966-1982	4.6%	6.9%	14.5%	13.2%
1982-2000	18.6%	18.6%	13.9%	18.0%
2000-2002	-17.8%	3.4%	-3.1%	-3.1%
Overall	10.0%	10.9%	10.8%	12.3%

The way it would work is that when P/R signaled that the end of the secular bull market was near in January 1999, one would shift to the 4-year rule. The four year rule would have one invested in stocks in early 1999, with a sell to come in December 2000. So one should stay fully invested in the market even after P/R reached record levels until December 2000. One would move out of stocks then and only re-enter the market in September 2002.

December 2000 was not a better time to exit the stock market than was September 1999 (when I made my final exit). The level of the market was about the same, and I would have given up the gains to be had in the income fund. But re-entering in September 2002 would have given me a much lower re-entry price than has my scale buying. Had I used the four-year rule, I would be about 20% ahead.

Stock investing outside the four year cycle

Now that I have learned of the four-year strategy one might ask why didn't I buy with the rest of my 401K in September 2002? The reason is that I was already committed to the scale buying strategy and I had already invested at higher levels. If the market goes further down (which is certainly possible) I need to take advantage of these levels with the funds I have left to gain the maximum reduction in my average cost basis. It will not be possible to reduce my average basis to as low as I would have if I invested 100% at September's monthly average. But a significant improvement could still be obtained.

Even if one has not previously committed funds to the market before learning about the four-year cycle, it doesn't do much good if one is not near one of the buying/selling points. A year from now the stock market could be much higher. It will then be obvious that an investment made in fall 2002 was a sound one. But that knowledge will not help an investor facing the decision of how to invest his 401K at that time. Finally, the four-year cycle is based on a historical pattern that has been observed for several decades. Prior to 1933, it did not work at all and even in the 1940's it didn't work all that well. Suppose it stops working in the future? The idea of 100% moves into and out of stocks using such a mechanical approach is somewhat unsettling. It requires a lot of faith. Many investors, especially those with some skill at stock picking, may wish to diversify strategies somewhat.

For those investors who have done well since 2000 there is no reason to change what has been successful so far. Others who had success prior to 2000 may have run into trouble since 2000, but still feel comfortable with their stock picking skill. For these investors I have presented evidence in the previous chapters suggesting that a new bull market either already began in October 2002, or will begin from marginally lower levels in 2003. The historical success of the four-year timing scheme and its apparent success in the current bear market are another argument in favor of this bull market scenario.

Actual examination of the historical record gives a less strongly bullish prognosis. Table 6.2 shows statistical projections of five-year returns from current levels as well as those of the recent past. The current position in the Stock Cycle is characterized in two ways, by the level of P/R and by the recent rate of change in this parameter. At the monthly average S&P500 value for October 2002, P/R was 0.77. At the previous major low in September 2001, P/R was 0.97. In January 2001, the two-year rate of change (ROC) in P/R first became negative and by June 2001, it had fallen below -10% annually. Using these parameters, several periods in the recent decline can be identified. Earliest is the period before March 2001, which is characterized by P/R above 1.17. The period between March and August 2001, excluding May, and that from October 2001 to May 2002 falls into a second category, P/R between 0.97 and 1.17 and showing a negative trend in P/R over the previous two years. A third category is defined by P/R between 0.77 and 0.97 and a trend of less than -10%/yr. The S&P entered this region in June 2002 and is still within it as of the end of March 2003. Should the S&P500 fall below its October low it will leave it on the downside, entering a yet lower valuation category also shown in Table 6.2. Should it rise much above 1000 or remain in this range of P/R until the end of 2003, it will also exit this region.

Table 6.2 Projected 5-year returns using two methods for various situations

P/R range	P/R 2-yr ROC	Price-based	Total Return-based
P/R > 1.17	any	0.5% (30%)	3.4% (73%)
0.97 < P/R ≤ 1.17	< 0%	0.4% (35%)	2.9% (65%)
0.77 ≤ P/R ≤ 0.97	< -10%	5.8% (85%)	9.2% (100%)
0.57 ≤ P/R < 0.77	< -10%	4.6% (75%)	8.3% (96%)

Table 6.2 shows projected five-year returns using two methods. The first employs the historical record of five-year capital gain returns that occurred under the P/R range and ROC listed. An estimated dividend yield of 1.6% is added for P/R > 1.17, of 2% for P/R less than 0.77 and 1.8% for those in between. The second method uses historical five-year total returns over the same eras. Also listed is the percentage of all the returns that exceeded an estimated 2% money market yield for the next five years.

The capital gain approach is a worst-case estimate in which it assumes that price gains today will be no different from those in the past, when dividends were greater. To the extent that a speculative nature remains in market psychology (which current valuations suggest is the case) it is quite possible that a greater proportion of total return in the coming years will come from capital gains than has historically been the case. If so, the historical total return example may give a better indication of future gains.

In either case, history suggests that past gains made from investments at current (November 2002) levels ought to produce a 5-9% return going forward, handily beating the money market return. Curiously, Table 6.2 suggests that expected returns for lower levels on the market would be *lower* than those expected today. This observation underscores the difficulty of using the historical record to forecast shorter term returns. In *Stock Cycles* I used rPR alone to forecast expected 20 year returns. Since rPR marks secular bull peaks, which are long-term by nature, it was easy to make useful forecasts for long-term returns. Attempting to do the same for short-term returns for narrowly defined eras reduces the range of historical eras from which the example data are drawn. The analysis in Table 6.2 should not be taken too literally. Basically, it suggests that intermediate-term stock index investments made at today's levels or lower are likely to produce modest returns going forward and will very likely beat today's very low money market rates.

Nothing in this analysis precludes much lower lows going forward, which if followed by a strong rally could still generate the modest 5-year returns suggested in Table 6.2. On the other hand, a modest return could be generated by a strong rally followed by another severe slump, so that the overall return is modest. After all, the 1997-2002 period has shown poor overall returns, yet shorter-term investments in the S&P500 were very profitable in 1997.

Gold and oil service stocks

Another investment strategy different from buying and selling the stock index is to invest in stocks whose value is determined largely by the value of an underlying commodity. Commodity-based stocks possess an investment merit not present with regular stocks. Since these stocks' price is based on an underlying commodity they should tend to follow the cycles of the commodity price (K-cycle) and not the stock market (Stock Cycle). Commodities had their great bull market during Kondratiev summer, when the stock market was in a secular bear market. Since the 1981 K-peak, commodities have been in a bear market, as is to be expected for a Kondratiev downwave, and so have remained range-bound rather than strongly rising as they did in the 1970's. This bear market in commodities should continue during the current downwave secular bear market in stocks. But since it has been going for more than 20 years, there has been a baseline of past activity that can be used to develop a trading rule. No similar rules can be obtained for other stocks (other than the four-year rule) since there has been no history of relevant performance.

Shares in gold mining companies are one particularly suitable type of commodity stock. The share prices of gold mining companies fluctuate with the price of gold. Rather than buying and selling the actual metal, one can buy the gold mining stocks instead. One way to do this is with a gold sector fund. The Fidelity Select Gold fund (FSAGX) is shown in Figure 6.1 as an example of gold stock performance. Chapter Four presented an analysis of gold as interpreted though the concept of monetary stimulation. The goal of this analysis was to determine a theoretical value for gold that could be used to determine when the metal was undervalued and when not. The idea would be to buy a portfolio of mining stocks or a gold stock fund when gold is undervalued and sell the stocks when gold advances above the model value.

Figure 6.1. Performance of gold stocks compared to the price of gold

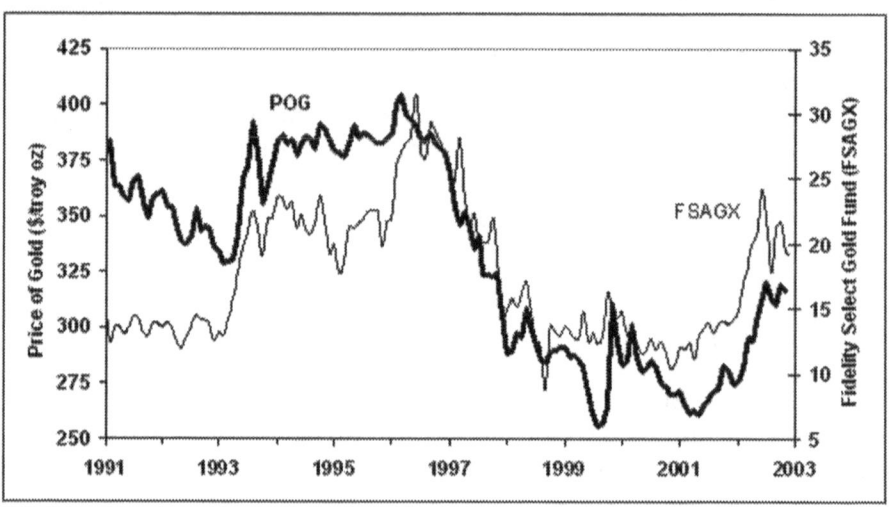

Another particularly suitable commodity with an associated class of stocks is oil. Stocks of companies engaged in oil and gas drilling or energy services in general show a great deal of volatility that is tied to the fluctuating price of oil. One way to invest in this entire sector is the Merrill Lynch Oil Service Holders Trust which trades on the American Stock Exchange under the symbol OIH. This holder is closely correlated with the Philadelphia Oil Service Index (OSX). Another way to invest in the sector generically is through an energy service sector fund such as the Fidelity Select Energy Service Fund (FSESX). Figure 6.2 shows a plot of an oil service stock index from 1986 to the present. This index consists of three entities spliced together: the Philadelphia Oil Service Index from 1997, the Fidelity Energy Services Fund for 1987 to 1997 and Halliburton Corporation stock (a major oil service stock) before 1987.

Figure 6.2 shows that oil service stocks show significant swings that in theory should be tradable. Two strategies were investigated to determine buy points for such a strategy. One involves buying oil stocks whenever the price per barrel of West Texas Intermediate (a grade of oil) falls below $16. Oil price data are available from the St. Louis Federal Reserve. The buying points obtained by this rule are shown in Figure 6.2 by the gray arrows. Another strategy involves buying whenever the rig count falls below 700. Rig count refers to the number of rotary drilling rigs currently in operation in the U.S. This figure is published weekly by the Baker-Hughes corporation and is available on their website (www.bakerhughes.com). Examination of Figure 6.2 shows that the rig-count method gave the better buy points over the 1986-2002 period.

Given a buying strategy one then needs a selling strategy. A simple strategy would be to put in a sell limit order when the total return exceeds a pre-determined amount. An example of a return rule might be a 50% annualized return in the 6-24 month period. For the first six months a threshold total return of 25% could be used. Whenever the price gain exceeds this return line, one puts in a limit order to sell at the return value. This limit is adjusted upward each month in accordance with the total return line. This strategy guarantees a 50% return for those positions closed within two years. Those positions not closed are sold at two years. Of the eight rig-based buys in Figure 6.2 all but two (those begun in Jan 1992 and May 1997) would have closed within two years. These positions, when closed at two years, would have generated 18% and 30% returns, respectively.

These returns look excellent, but one must consider that to obtain them one must have funds outside the market waiting to be deployed. There is an opportunity cost of doing this. When the money-market returns obtained while waiting to buy oil stocks are factored in, the overall returns obtainable from such a strategy fall into the 16-19% range, as compared to about 18% obtained from a passive stock index investment. Thus, the superior returns obtained from the well-timed oil stock investments were countered by the opportunity cost of being out of stocks during a secular bull market.

Figure 6.2 The oil stock index (1986-present)

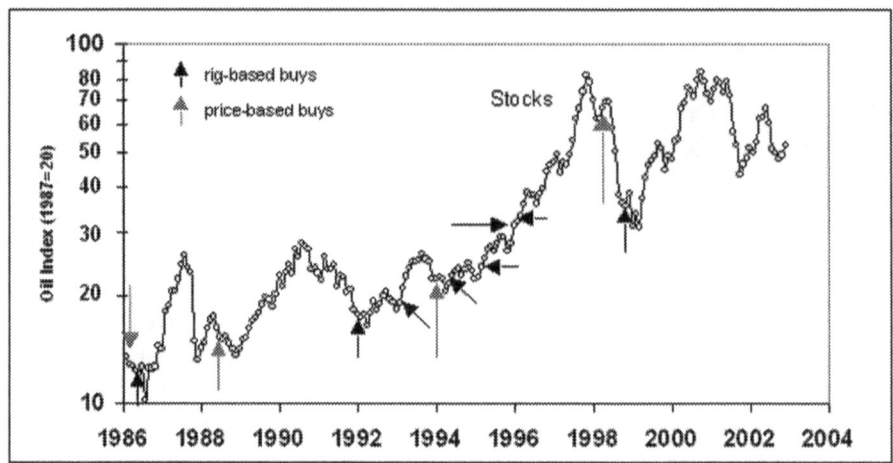

During a secular bear market this opportunity cost is much less. If a 2% return is assumed for a typical money market return for the present secular bear market, the timing strategy described above wold be expected to return about 11-14%, which is comparable to the return obtained by the four-year cycle strategy in the last secular bear market. About half of the rig-based buys in Figure 6.2 occurred during a time in which one would already be fully-invested according to the four-year rule. Thus, this strategy provides additional investment opportunities outside those provided by the four-year cycle.

This strategy assumes that the same sort of oscillations that occurred in oil service stocks during the secular bull market will continue into the secular bear market. There are a number of reasons for believing that this will happen. One is the speculative nature of investors in the early stages of as secular bear market. Investors will actively seek return and will aggressively buy stocks that promise to do this. Furthermore, they will be quick to sell them if they don't perform. Another is the non-inflationary nature of the current secular bear market, in which earnings growth will be the determinant of stock prices. Earnings will depend on revenue, which is a function of the number of active rigs. Since the strategy is based on the number of rigs in operation, it is linked to the fundamentals driving earnings of the drilling business.

Another reason is shown by Figure 6.3. Oil prices were largely flat from the late 1940's to 1973. Drilling activity showed a long-term decline over the second half of the 1950's and 1960's. This reflected the gradual discovery of all the easy-to-find oil in the U.S. Total output continued to grow despite falling drilling activity until the early 1970's, when production peaked. During this entire time, increasing U.S. production served to keep a cap on the price of oil. By 1973, U.S. production could no longer serve this function and OPEC was able to obtain enormous price increases in 1973 and in 1979. As prices rose, the revenue obtainable from declining US oil production soared. This windfall led to vastly increased drilling activity as shown by the exponentially-rising rig count throughout the 1970's.

Figure 6.3. Oil price, reduced price and rig count 1955-present

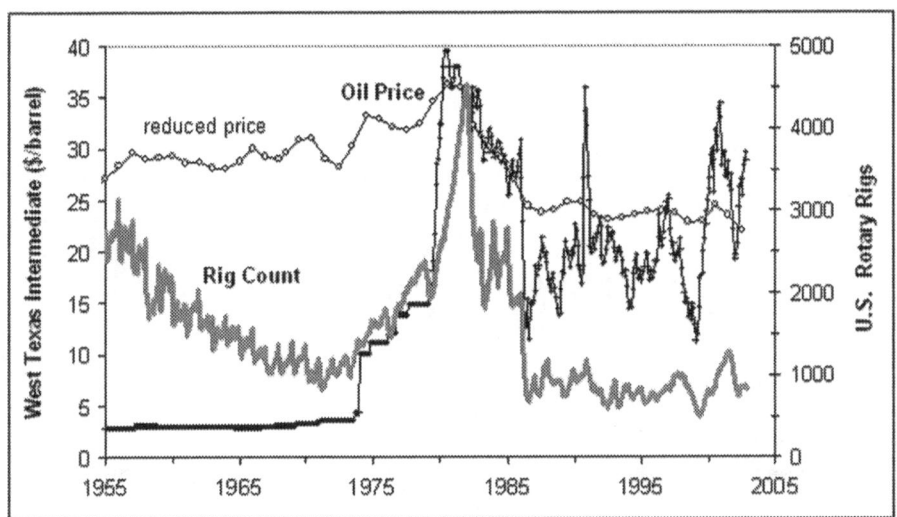

The soaring oil prices were a consequence of Kondratiev summer, a time during which commodity prices of all types tend to rise dramatically. Oil prices peaked in 1980, around the time of the Kondratiev peak in reduced price (Figure 6.3). After the peak, prices moderated and then collapsed at the Kitchen cycle bottom in 1986. Drilling activity followed suit. It is clear that since 1973 drilling activity (and hence the profit potential for oil-service companies) has depended on price. Like any other commodity price, oil will follow the K-cycle. As long as the downwave persists, commodity prices will experience a downward bias, which will be offset by rising stimulus. Thus, as long as reduced price continues to fall, oil prices should remain range-bound as they have been since the early 1980's. This means drilling activity should follow suit and the type of buying rule developed earlier should continue to hold.

Figure 6.4 shows a graph of the stock index and oil prices since 1986. In general stock prices do tend to follow oil price. However the timing can be off.

Consider the behavior in early 1998, when oil price plummeted below $16 a barrel, which is a very low price as shown in Figure 6.4. Despite this low oil price, the stock index was still very high. It eventually fell to very low levels, but had one employed a $16 per barrel rule one would have bought stocks far too soon. Figure 6.5 shows that drilling activity declined considerably later than oil prices, not penetrating the 700 rig "buy" level until October 1998, by which time stocks had already completed most of their eventual decline.

Figure 6.4. Stock index versus oil price 1986-present

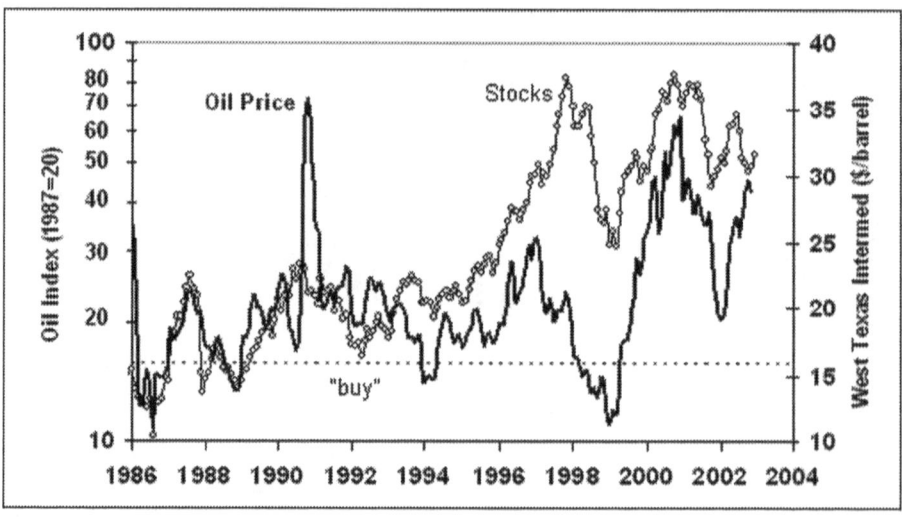

At the recent low in rig count in March 2002, rig count fell to about 10% above the 700 buy level. At this low in rig count, the stock index was close to a peak value. Clearly March 2002 would have been a poor time to buy. The oil price was high (around $26/barrel) in March 2002, which is not suggestive of a good time to buy oil stocks. Looking at all the previous rig-based buys one finds that all of them occurred at times when oil prices were less than $20 a barrel. Thus, a corollary might be added to the 700 rig rule that oil prices be less than $20 a barrel.

Since the 700 rig level wasn't breached in spring 2002, one might ask why a corollary is necessary. The reason is the fall from plateau. Such a drop in reduced price would be similar to the 1981-86 drop (Figure 6.3). This period also saw a significant permanent drop in rig counts as well as a sharp decline in price. Should something like this accompany the fall from plateau, there is a risk of buying high. It is therefore prudent to make sure that stock purchases made during this volatile period be made at the lower end of *both* rig count and oil price.

Examination of the P/E's of selected oil driller stocks shows a median value in the low 30's. This is rather high for a cyclical stock like a driller. Should the general stock market pick up (as is expected, based on the four-year rule) one would expect these multiples to fall as non-cyclical stocks find favor. In my opinion, the extra protection obtained with the $20 price corollary is warranted by both the uncertainty of the fall from plateau and the worrisome current valuation.

For more knowledgeable investors, I suggest scale-buying of a portfolio of individual oil driller stocks beginning around the time an index buy is indicated by the 700 rig + $20 price rule. By studying the company's financials, one can select three or four good companies to buy instead of a broad-based fund. Selection of good companies can improve return by eliminating dogs, and scale buying can improve the average price obtained. But doing this requires some skill in both financial and technical analysis.

Figure 6.5 Stock index versus rig count 1986-present

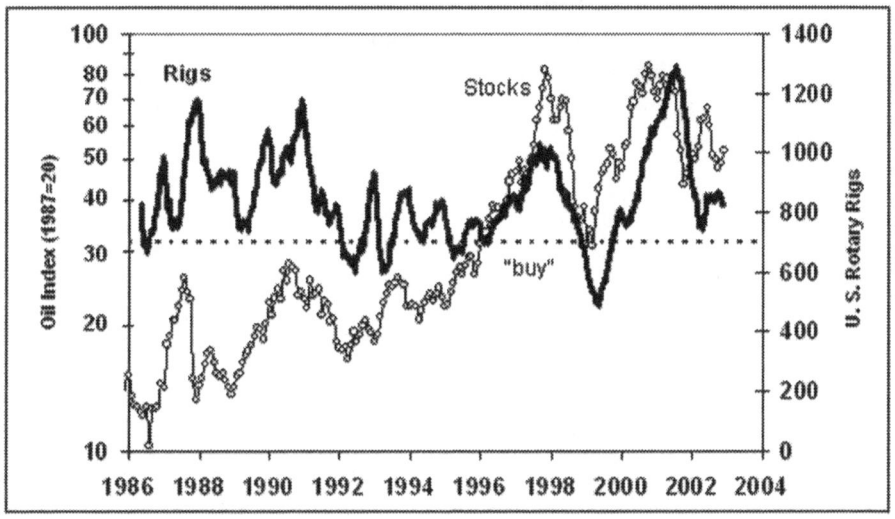

There may be an opportunity to exploit a mismatch between stimulation and commodity price that should develop with the fall from plateau. In the long run stimulation will drive up the price of commodities like gold and oil. But with the deflationary tendencies of the fall from plateau it should be possible to still see low commodity prices going forward (and to buy the associated stocks). At this point these stocks would be undervalued relative to their long-term future in much the same way as ordinary stocks are in the late stages of secular bear markets. Thus, even if oil or gold stocks purchased in accordance with the rules developed here were to fall lower in price, one can be confident that in time, stimulation will force oil and gold prices much higher, producing an acceptable return. That is, at the levels suggested here, oil and gold stocks would be long-term undervalued, in contrast to ordinary stocks, which are not.

There is then fairly little risk of loss by buying a *diversified* portfolio of oil or gold stocks at the levels given in this chapter for oil stocks or in chapter four for gold stocks. It is thus not recommended to automatically sell any stocks purchased after two years if their return has not yet met the sell criterion. It is probably better to wait for the long-term trend to carry them higher.

To summarize, for the current secular bear market, a reasonable oil-strategy would be to buy an oil index, mutual fund, or diversified portfolio of oil service stocks should the Baker-Hughes rig count fall below 700 while the price of West Texas intermediate is below $20 per barrel. An appropriate sell rule might be a flat 25% gain in the first six months, a 50% annualized return for 6-24 months, a flat 125% gain for 2-4.5 years, and a 20% annualized return for periods longer than 4.5 years. A reasonable gold strategy would be to buy gold stocks when gold is about 10% below the model value in Chapter 4 and put in a trailing stop when the gold price rises 10% above the model value.

Chapter 7

Charting the Course of the
Secular Bear Market

In this final chapter, I use historical patterns in P/R to sketch out a rough path for the S&P500 index during this secular bear market. The final product of this analysis is the figure shown in Chapter 1. Of course, it is impossible to predict the market's precise future behavior. What one can do is use the general properties of secular bear markets to identify approximate boundaries within which the market will likely wander. This idea is then combined with the general tendency of the market to move in trends, which suggests that lengthy bear market periods during which the general trend is down will be followed by bull market periods when the trend is up. Approximately three to five such oscillations will make up the complete secular bear market era.

So far, we are in the third year of the first ordinary bear market in the post-2000 secular bear market. At some point this bear market will end and a bull market will begin. This bull market will in time also end and be followed by a second bear market. Several of these bull/bear market cycles will be completed until a final bear market bottom sometime around 2018 will end the secular bear market era.

Figure 7.1 Bull/bear market oscillations in P/R during past secular bear markets

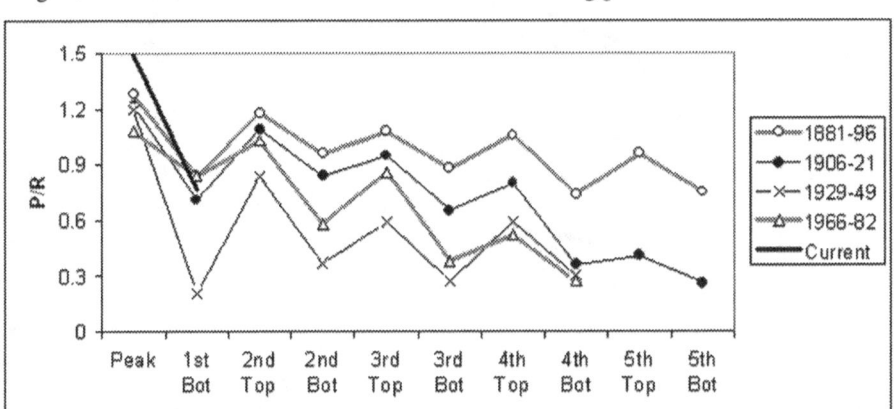

Figure 7.1 shows the progress of previous secular bear markets in terms of maximum and minimum P/R values during the bull/bear market cycles embedded within the secular trend. P/R declines during the entire secular bear market era. It begins at the highest level and ends at (close to) the low-est level of the entire secular bear market era. With one exception, the bull/bear cycle lows early in the secular bear market era are higher than are those later in the era. The same is true of the bull/bear cycle highs. With one exception, P/R at the end of the secular bear market is quite low (around 0.3), especially when compared to the level at the beginning of the secular bear market.

One can combine the data in Figure 7.1 with a projected trend for R to obtain an estimate of the approximate ranges for the tops and bottoms of the bull/bear market cycles to come during the present secular bear market. Figure 7.2 shows a plot of the S&P500 from 1997 through the end of 2002. Also shown are projected bull market highs and bear market lows based on those seen in three of the four most recent secular bear market eras. The Great Depression secular bear market was not used. These projections were obtained by extrapolating the 4.5% growth rate for R over the past three years into the future, and then applying the high and low values for P/R from Figure 7.1 to obtain lower and upper bounds for bull/bear cycle highs and lows. This same sort of approach was used to construct Figure 1.1.

Figure 7.2. Projected bull/bear market extremes for the near future.

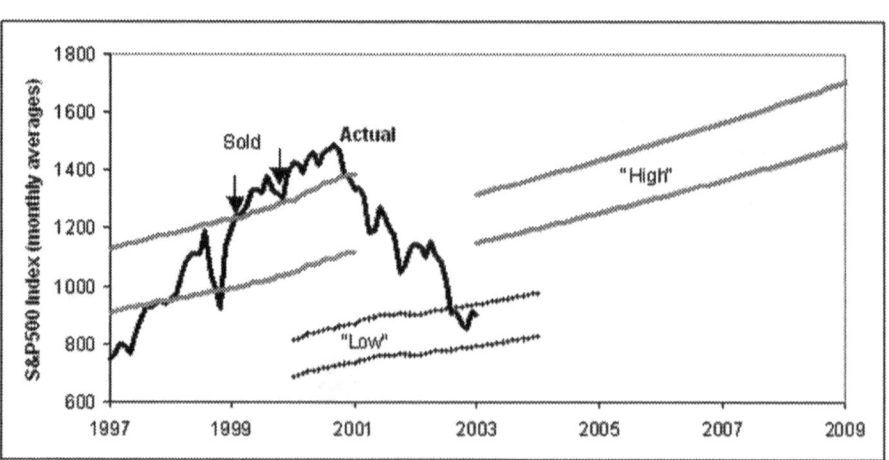

The first set of limits were those used to time the bull market peak in the late 1990's. As I described earlier, I sold out in late 1998 through late summer 1999 as P/R reached and exceeded previous all-time highs. I had waited for all-time highs because of the stimulatory effect I expected from the 1997 capital gains reduction. In actuality, stocks went somewhat higher than the projections. Since peaking in 2000, stocks entered a bear market and (so far) have fallen to levels consistent with the initial bear market of three of the four previous secular bear markets. This has been discussed in Chapter Three. At some point this bear market will end and a new bull market begin. Based on the P/R levels reached in the second top from these same three secular bear markets (see Figure 7.1) a window for the top of the coming bull market can be projected. One could use these levels to begin a selling program similar to that which I executed in 1999.

Had I employed the four-year cycle strategy described in the previous chapter there would be no need to construct projections like that in Figure 7.2. I would simply plan to sell in December 2004. But since I did not follow this strategy and I bought back into the market too early I may not want to sell in December 2004. If the S&P500 is still well below around 1400 or so, as seems likely, I will probably not sell, in the expectation of substantially higher highs during the next four year cycle.

Figure 7.3 shows one of the risks of this analysis. This figure was constructed in exactly the same fashion as Figure 7.2, except the P/R limits from the Great Depression secular bear market were included. In this figure the "low" range is much wider that in the previous figure reflecting the very low P/R of 1932. The much lower bull market valuations from the Depression are also reflected in the range projections for the high values for the next bull market peak. This figure shows a very different picture of the investment terrain over the next few years. Stocks could be only slightly higher than today half a decade hence, after having fallen a long way in between. As described in Chapter Three, this situation is exactly what is to be expected based on conventional valuation measures such as Tobin's Q. It is the bearish story told by these indicators that has allowed the market to have fallen as far as it already has with no panic or crash. And it is the bearish story that they continue to tell that makes investing at today's levels so scary.

Figure 7.3. Alternate projected bull/bear market extremes for the present decade

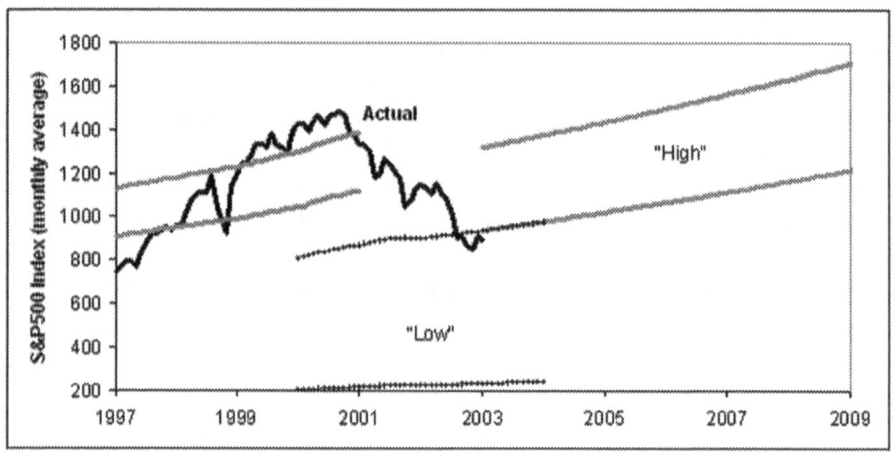

By comparing Figure 7.2 with Figure 7.3 one can see why it is necessary to obtain additional information from auxiliary cycles before making an investment decision based on projections for future returns. Investment in the S&P500 at today's levels (ca. 800's) is likely to be quite profitable provided the future course of the market will more closely resemble the story told by Figure 7.2 than the story told by Figure 7.3. This is the purpose for characterizing the Kuznets cycle in Chapter Two and for developing the reduced price concepts in Chapter Four. The former shows that the Kuznets cycle is still moving up during the current secular bear market rather than down as it was for the Depression secular bear market. And the reduced price analysis shows that outright deflation will not likely occur in this secular bear market, unlike the situation during the Depression. This analysis provides the confidence that the story told by Figure 7.2, not Figure 7.3, is the correct one.

Using the projections to aid investment decisions

Once it is assumed that Figure 7.2 is the more likely scenario, the next issue is to determine how to act on the information. Had one been following the four-year cycle methodology described in the last chapter, one would already be fully invested in stocks. In my own case my 401K is 80% allocated to stocks, and this allocation will be increased should the S&P500 fall to or below its October 2002 low. It is important to realize that just as the previous bull market exceeded the projections in Figure 7.2, so can the current bear market.

Nevertheless, reducing stock allocation in the middle of the late 1990's high region would have still provided a superior investment result compared to continuation of a full-invested posture. Similarly, it is expected that purchasing the S&P500 within the "low" guidelines (below ~940 on the S&P500 for early 2003) will provide an adequate return going forward. Buying at lower levels is of course better. Eventually a new bull market will get underway and the S&P500 will move well above the "low" region in Figure 7.2. As the market moves into the "high" region in Figure 7.2, purchases of stocks are no longer a good idea, although selling existing stocks is not necessarily warranted.

Since one cannot know when a minor decline is really the start of something bigger, decisions to sell cannot easily be made after stocks have started to decline. For example, one could have sold stocks in October 1998, based on the fact that the S&P500 index had already reached the "high" level and had started a serious decline (see Figure 7.2). This would have been a mistake. Selling in 1999 (as I did) or in December 2000 in accordance with the four-year strategy would have been a better decision.

One selling strategy would be to reduce stock allocation in December 2004, when the four year cycle suggests one do so. Selling allows one to take advantage of future buying opportunities. The higher the index moves in 2004, the greater the likelihood that the buying opportunity in 2006 will be good. Selling in accordance with the four-year rule would allow one to book paper capital gains at the cost of missing out on further rises. Had one bought in 2002 according to the four-year rule, it is likely these gains will be large.

But there is no certainty that the four-year rule will "work" for each cycle. What the historical evidence suggests is if pursued as an overall strategy, it will work often enough to give a better return than buy-and-hold. The advantage the four-year cycle has already gained in the current cycle is so great that it need not outperform a buy-and-hold strategy for the rest of this secular bear market and still provide the same sort of superior result it has in past secular bear markets. It is entirely possible that the S&P500 could be higher in October 2006 (when the four-year method would signal a buy) than it was in Dec 2004 (when the method signals a sell). If one does not have large capital gains going into 2004, use of the four-year cycle strategy to sell is less appealing.

Another selling strategy would be to sell if a likely superior alternate investment is available. Assuming that Figure 7.2 gives an approximate picture of what to expect in the next few years, one can conclude that levels above 1400 on the S&P500 are likely to occur *sometime* in this decade. Assuming the 1400 level is reached by Dec 2008 (the next four-year sell point after 2004), one can calculate an estimated return based on the current date and level of the S&P500. For example, consider the situation in which the S&P500 were to reach 1200 in late 2004. This level is within the "high" levels in Figure 7.2 and late 2004 is close to a "sell" point called for by the four-year rule. Assuming a level of 1400 should be achievable within four years and adding 2% dividends implies a likely return of 6% could be obtained from this level. Unless bond yields are well above 6% in 2004, one would likely be better off in stocks and one would not sell. Should stocks rise further, say to 1300 by late 2004, the anticipated return now falls to a level at which bond yields as low 5% can compete. Obviously, if an extreme level like 1400 were to be reached in 2004, shifting out of stocks would be recommended almost regardless of bond yields.

In any case, investment of additional funds in the stock index would not be recommended in 2004. Additional index investments should wait for the next four year buy point in fall 2006. Bonds are an option if the yield meets your required return needs. If the expansion continues to the next Kichen cycle top in ~2008 interest rates will likely rise after 2004. This would mean that bond investments made in 2004 may have to be held until the next recession in order to get a capital gain, thus the yield received in the meantime should be adequate to justify tying up assets for this period of time. Of course oil and gold opportunities can arise at any time and the wait to 2006 is not so long that perhaps simply parking the assets in a money market or similar liquid investment may be acceptable.

With this I finish my discussion of secular bear markets dynamics and investment strategies. Any projection extending beyond the next bull/bear market cycle is really premature at this point. It is still too early to know whether historical analogy is truly a useful tool to aid investment decisions.

Conclusions

A fitting conclusion might be to summarize the predictions that have been made in this book. Future readers can then assess the accuracy of the predictions to directly assess the utility of the historical methods described here.

1. We are in a secular bear market. Specifically, this means the S&P500 should not move sustainably above the March 2000 peak on a constant dollar basis until after 2018.

2. The bear market that began this secular bear market in March 2000 probably ended on October 9, 2002. The S&P500 is not expected to fall significantly below the 776 level reached then. So far, it has not (the lowest it has closed since October is about 800 on March 11, 2003.

3. The housing market should remain strong until next year (2004) or maybe even later. A double-dip recession shouldn't happen.

4. The market should return to the neighborhood of its old highs before this expansion is over.

5. Interest rates should fall substantially in the next recession and not come back up afterward even if inflation picks up.

As time goes on the accuracy of these predictions will become known and with it the utility of the methodology used to make them. But for now, there can be no assurance that the methodology is reliable.

References

1. Alexander, Michael A. (2000a) *Stock cycles: why stocks won't beat money markets over the next twenty years*, Writers Club Press, 2000.

2. Alexander, Michael A. (2000b) post dated August 21, 2000 in "The Kondratiev Wave and the Fourth Turning" on *The Fourth Turning* website (www.fourthturning.com/cgi-bin/netforum/thefuture/a.cgi).

3. Alexander, Michael A (2001), "Use of Secular Trend Concept for Asset Allocation in 401K", web article on Safehaven.com (www.safehaven.com), May 26, 2001.

4. Alexander, Michael A. (2002a), *The Kondratiev Cycle*, Writers Club Press, 2002.

5. Alexander, Michael A (2002b), "Use of Secular Trend Concept for Asset Allocation in 401K Update", web article on Safehaven.com (www.safehaven.com), April 16, 2002.

6. Alexander, Michael A (2002c), "Use of Secular Trend Concept for Asset Allocation in 401K Part 3", web article on Safehaven.com (www.safehaven.com), July 15, 2002.

7. Alexander, Michael A (2002d), "Progress Update on the Current Secular Bear Market", web article on Safehaven.com (www.safehaven.com), July 23, 2002.

8. Alexander, Michael A. (2000e) post dated August 25, 2002 on the *Longwaves* website (www.longwaves.net).

9. Alexander, Michael A (2002f), "How Low Can We Go? What Several Valuation Methods Have to Say", web article on Safehaven.com (www.safehaven.com), October 20, 2002.

10. Arnold, Curtis M., *Timing the market*, Chicago: Probus Publishing, 1993.

11. Bernanke, Benjamin S., remarks before the National Economists Club, Washington, D.C., November 21, 2002 (www.federalreserve.gov/boarddocs/speeches/2002).

12. Berry, Brian J., *Long-wave rhythms in economic development and political behavior*, Baltimore: The Johns Hopkins University Press, 1991.

13. Bronson, Robert E., "A Forecasting Model That Integrates Multiple Business and Stock-Market Cycles", web article at Safehaven.com (www.safehaven.com), August 12, 2002.

14. Bureau of the Census, housing data (www.census.gov/const/uspricemon.pdf)

15. Dent, Harry S., *The Great Boom Ahead*, New York: Hyperion 1993.

16. Dent, Harry S., *The Roaring 2000s: Building the wealth and life style you desire in the greatest boom in history*, New York: Simon and Schuster, 1998.

17. Federal Reserve Bank of St. Louis at www.economagic.com

18. Federal Reserve Bank of St. Louis, WTI oil prices: (http://research.stlouisfed.org/fred/data/business/oilprice)

19. Furfero, A. Joyce, *Macroeconomic Stabilization Policies: Goals, Institutions and Theories*, 8th ed. September 1, 2000. (www.drfurfero.com/books/231book/ch03d.html)

20. Gaffney, Mason, "Privatizing Land Without Giveaway", Delivered at Conference on Social Collection of Rent in the Soviet Union, New York City, August 22-24, 1990. (www.earthrights.net/docs/privatize.html)

21. Garcia, René, and Pierre Perron (1995), "An Analysis of the Real Interest Rate Under Regime Shifts", *Scientific Series*, No. 95s-5, CIRANO—Centre Interuniversitaire de Recherché en Analyse des Organisations.

22. Geanakoplos, John, Michael Magill, and Martine Quinzii, "Demography and the Long-Run Predictability of the Stock Market," USC CLEO Research Paper No. C02-21; Cowles Foundation Discussion Paper No. 1380, August 2002, available from SSRN (http://papers.ssrn.com).

23. Global Financial Data (www.globalfindata.com).

24. Goertzel, Ted, (2000) "Generational Cycles in Mass Psychology: Implications for the George W. Bush Administration" (www.crab.rutgers.edu/~goertzel/cycles.htm)

25. Hamilton, James D., (1989), "A New Approach to the Economic Analysis of NonStationary Time Series and the Business Cycle", *Econometrica*, 57(2) 357-384.

26. Homer Hoyt, "The Urban Real Estate Cycle—Performances and Prospects", Urban Land Institute Technical Bulletin No. 38, June 1960, in *According to Hoyt: 53 years of Homer Hoyt*, no publisher, 1970.

27. HR Consultants, *The Four Year Stock Market Cycle*, webpage (cpcug.org/user/invest/fouryear.html).

28. Clement Juglar, *Des Crises commerciales et leur retour periodique en France, en Angleterre, et aux Etats-Unis*, 1862.

29. Joseph Kitchin, "Cycles and Trends in Economic Policy," *Review of Economic Statistics*, Jan. 1923.

30. Kolari, James W and Ariel M. Viale, "Gibson or Fisher Paradox? Back to the Future Expectations and Escape Dynamics of a Very Plausible Robust Agent", 2001, unpublished manuscript.

31. Simon Kuznets, Secular Movements in Production and Prices, 1930.

32. Lebergott, Stanley, *Manpower in Economic Growth, The American Experience Since 1800*, NewYork: McGraw-Hill 1964.

33. Lichello, Robert, *How to Make a 1,000,000 in the Stock Market Automatically!*, Signet Books, 1977

34. McFadden, David, "Demographics, the housing market, and the welfare of the elderly", in David A. Wise (ed) *Studies in the Economics of Aging*, Chicago: University of Chicago Press, 1994.

35. Mitchell, B. P. *International Historical Statistics: The Americas 1750-1993*, New York: Stockton Press, 1998.

36. National Association of Realtors (www.realtor.org).

37. Ohio State University, Fisher College of Business (www.cob.ohio-state.edu/~fin/resources_data/data).

38. Roper, Don, and Lori Warner, (1991), "Late Nineteenth Century U.S. Monetary Controversy: Reinterpreting the Easy Money Forces" (csf.colorado.edu/authors/Roper.Don/bimetallism.pdf)

39. Roper, Don, and Lance Girton (1993), "Gold Debt and the Great Depression", (csf.colorado.edu/authors/Roper.Don/gold-deb.pdf)

40. Rothchild, John, *The Bear Book: Survive and Profit in Ferocious Markets*, New York: John Wiley and Sons, 1998.

41. Schwartz, Peter and Peter Leyden, "The long boom: a history of the future, 1980-2020", *Wired*, July 1997.

42. Shiller, Robert J. *Irrational Exuberance*, Princeton NJ: Princeton University Press, 2000.

43. Smithers, Andrew and Stephen Wright, *Valuing Wall Street: Protecting Wealth in Turbulent Markets*, New York: McGraw-Hill, 2000.

44. Strauss, William and Neil Howe, *Generations: The History of America's Future 1584 to 2069*, New York: Quill William Morrow 1991.

45. Strauss, William and Neil Howe, (1997a) *The Fourth Turning*, New York: Broadway Books, 1997.

46. Strauss, William and Neil Howe, (1997b) *The Fourth Turning*, 1997, website (www.fourthturning.com)

47. U.S. Department of Treasury monthly statement (www.fms.treas.gov/mts/index.html)

Appendix A. Identifying Business Cycles

The National Bureau of Economic Research (NBER) has identified US business cycles back to 1854. Prior to then one can use the GDP relative to its trend as a crude estimate for cycles. Figure A.1 shows GDP divided by its 25-year trend value. The trend value is the value obtained from regression of log GDP versus time over a 25 year period centered on the year of interest. Thus the trend for a point in 1853 is regression of data over 1840 to 1865. For points before 1803, the regression equation for the 1790-1815 period was used.

Also shown in the figure as the thick light-gray line is the Kondratiev seasonal cycle. This cycle is a binary subharmonic of the Kondratiev cycle (two seasonal cycles per K-cycle) and is correlated with the stock cycle. It is the same cycle that Bronson calls the BAAC Supercycle. I used a plot analogous to Figure A.1, but using a 100 year trend, to show this cycle in my book *The Kondratiev Cycle* (p 67).

Figure A.1 GDP relative to 25-yr trend showing K-seasonal and ordinary business cycles

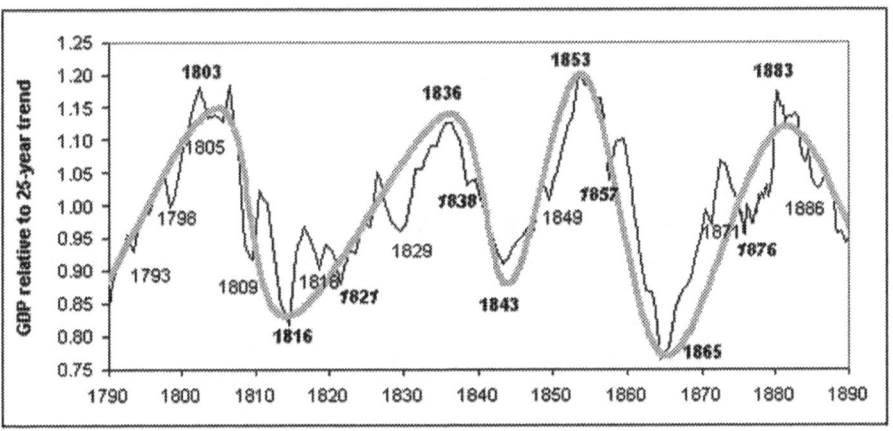

Within the larger seasonal cycles, there are smaller perturbations, which presumably reflect ordinary business cycles. In *The Kondratiev Cycle* I smoothed these to de-emphasize them and bring out the longer cycle. Now I wish to examine these shorter cycles. Recession troughs are marked by visual inspection. Four troughs (marked in ***bold italics***) are the recessions associated with the four big "panics" that occurred during the period shown in the chart: the panics of 1819, 1837, 1857 and 1873. The others are either "major" troughs or isolated ones. Figure A.2 shows more cycles for the period 1880-1950.

To test the validity of these troughs I compared them with those obtained by NBER. Table A.1 shows troughs from Figures A.1 and A.2 compared to the NBER recession bottoms. The correspondence is quite good. All but three NBER recessions have a corresponding trough and only one trough doesn't have an associated NBER recession. This suggests that the business cycles obtained from Figure A.1 can be used to provide estimates for business cycle dates before 1854. Table A.2 lists all the business cycles from 1787 to the present.

Figure A.2. K-seasonal and ordinary business cycles 1880-1950

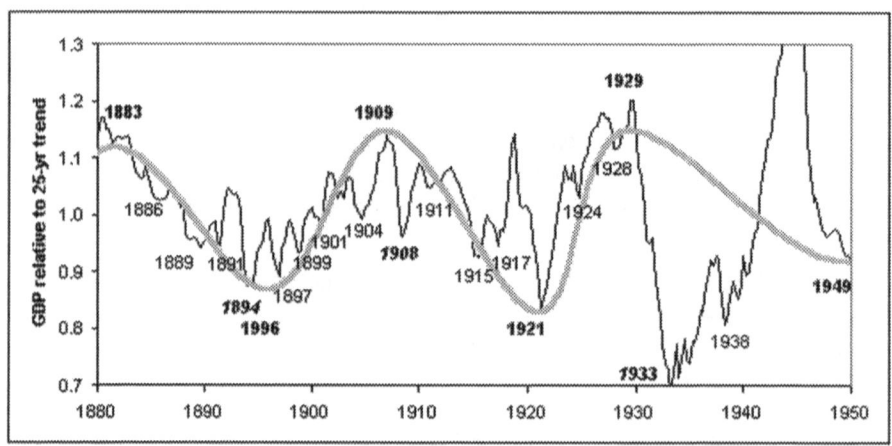

Table A.1 GDP troughs from Figures B.1 and B.2 compared to NBER recession bottoms

NBER recession	GDP trough	NBER recession	GDP trough	NBER recession	GDP trough
Dec 1854	–	Jun 1894	1894	Mar 1919	1917
Dec 1858	1857	Jun 1897	1897	Jul 1921	1921
Jun 1861	–	–	1899	Jul 1924	1924
Dec 1867	1865	Dec 1900	1901	Nov 1927	1928
Dec 1870	1871	Aug 1904	1904	Apr 1933	1933
Mar 1879	1876	Jun 1908	1908	Jun 1938	1938
May 1885	1886	Jan 1912	1911	Oct 1945	–
Apr 1888	1889	Dec 1914	1915	Oct 1949	1949
Apr 1891	1891				

Table A.2. Kondratiev seasonal cycles and their associated business cycles

K-seasons[1]	Business Cycle[1]	K-seasons[1]	Business Cycle[1]
1787-1802	**1787**-1792 (E)	**1897**-1910	Jun **1897**-Jun 1899 (E)
(Spring)	1792-1793 (R)	(Spring)	Jun 1899-Dec 1900 (R)
	1793-1797 (E)		Dec 1900-Sep 1902 (E)
	1797-1798 (R)		Sep 1902-Aug 1904 (R)
	1798-1802(E)		Aug 1904-May 1907 (E)
1802-1818	1802-1805 (R)		May 1907-Jun 1908 (R)
(Summer)	1805-1806 (E)		Jun 1908-Jan 1910 (E)
	1806-1809 (R)	1910-1921	Jan 1910-Jan 1912 (R)
	1809-1810 (E)	(Summer)	Jan 1912-Jan 1913 (E)
	1810-1814 (R)		Jan 1913-Dec 1914 (R)
	1814-*1816* (E)		Dec 1914-Aug 1918 (E)
	1816-1818 (R)		Aug 1918-Mar 1919 (R)
1818-1836	1818-1819 (E)		Mar 1919-Jan *1920* (E)
(Fall)	1819-1821 (R)		Jan *1920*-Jul 1921 (R)
	1821-1826 (E)	1921-1929	Jul 1921-May 1923 (E)
	1826-1829 (R)	(Fall)	May 1923-Jul 1924 (R)
	1829-1836 (E)		Jul 1924-Oct 1926 (E)
1836-**1843**	1836-1838 (R)		Oct 1926-Nov 1927 (R)
(Winter)	1838-1839 (E)		Nov 1927-Aug 1929 (E)
	1839-**1843** (R)	1929-1949	Aug 1929-Apr 1933 (R)
1843-1853	**1843**-1848 (E)	(Winter)	Apr 1933-May 1937 (E)
(Spring)	1848-1849 (R)		May 1937-Jun 1938 (R)
	1849-1853 (E)		Jun 1938-Feb 1945 (E)
1853-1867	1853-Dec 1854 (R)		Feb 1945-Oct 1945 (R)
(Summer)	Dec 1854-Jun 1857 (E)		Oct 1945-Nov 1948 (E)
	Jun 1857-Dec 1858 (R)		Nov 1948-Oct **1949** (R)
	Dec 1858-Oct 1860 (E)	**1949**-1968	Oct **1949**-Jul 1953 (E)
	Oct 1860-Jun 1861 (R)	(Spring)	Jul 1953-May 1954 (R)
	Jun 1861-Apr *1865* (E)		May 1954-Aug 1957 (E)
	Apr *1865*-Dec 1867 (R)		Aug 1957-Apr 1958 (R)
1867-1882	Dec 1867-Jun 1869 (E)		Apr 1958-Apr 1960 (E)
(Fall)	Jun 1869-Dec 1870 (R)		Apr 1960-Feb 1961 (R)
	Dec 1870-Oct 1873 (E)		Feb 1961-Dec 1969 (E)
	Oct 1873-Mar 1879 (R)	1969-1982	Dec 1969-Nov 1970 (R)
	Mar 1879-Mar 1882 (E)	(Summer)	Nov 1970-Nov 1973 (E)

K-seasons[1]	Business Cycle[1]	K-seasons[1]	Business Cycle[1]
1882-**1897**	Mar 1882-May 1885 (R)		Nov 1973-Mar 1975 (R)
(Winter)	May 1885-May 1887 (E)		Mar 1975-Jan 1980 (E)
	Mar 1887-Apr 1888 (R)		Jan 1980-Jul 1980 (R)
	Apr 1888-Jul 1890 (E)		Jul 1980-Jul *1981* (E)
	Jul 1890-Apr 1891 (R)		Jul *1981*-Nov 1982 (R)
	Apr 1891-Dec 1893 (E)	1982-2001	Nov 1982-Jul 1990 (E)
	Dec 1893-Jun 1894 (R)	(Fall)	Jul 1990-Mar 1991 (R)
	Jun 1894-Dec 1895 (E)		Mar 1991-Mar 2001 (E)
	Dec 1895-Jun **1897** (R)	2001-	Mar 2001- (R)

[1]   Years in ***bold italics*** denote Kondratiev peaks, those in plain **bold**, Kondratiev troughs

Appendix B. Defining Bear Markets

Bear markets are usually considered as "large" declines in the stock index over a fairly lengthy period of time. A common rule of thumb is any decline of 20% or greater. The market analyst Robert Bronson (2002) has developed novel measure of bear market severity which I will make use of here (see exhibit E in Bronson article). This method accounts for both the magnitude and the length of the bear market decline and is defined as follows:

B.1   Severity = log(index top/index bottom) x duration in months

For example, the current bear market, which began at the S&P500 intra-day peak of 1552.87 on March 24, 2000, has reached (so far) an intra-day low of 768.63 on October 10, 2002. Through the October low, the bear market has lasted 30.5 months. From this data I can calculate a severity as follows:

B.2   Severity = log(1552.87/768.63) x 30.5 = 9.3.

Bronson (2002, exhibit E) lists thirty bear markets since 1895 as assessed by this criterion. Already the present bear market falls into the #2 position in his list, and it may not yet be over. The nature of this measure can make fairly small declines significant bear markets—if they last long enough. For example, the short, but severe, 1987 bear market showed a decline 150% greater than the much longer 1960 bear market, yet was 40% less severe by the Bronson criterion. This makes identification of major bear markets more difficult than the use of the simple 20% rule.

Some of the bear markets in Bronson's list seem pretty small. For example the 1926 bear market has a severity of only 0.12. One can find declines not on his list with greater severity. For example, the 12% Dow decline from July 15, 1943 to November 30, 1943 (severity = 0.25); the 10.8% S&P500 decline from Sept 25, 1967 to March 5, 1968 (severity = 0.26); or the 13.9% S&P500 decline from April 29, 1971 to November 24, 1971 (severity = 0.45).

None of these declines fits the 20% standard, but they all are more severe (by the Bronson definition) than the 1926 bear market, yet are not included in the list of top bear markets. The 1926 bear market was associated with an NBER recession dated from October 1926 to November 1927, whereas none of the larger declines mentioned above were associated with recessions. If special significance is assigned to those bear markets associated with recessions, the inclusion of the 1926 bear, but none of the others mentioned above can be justified as significant bear markets. Only one of Bronson's non-recession bear markets did not show 20% decline, that in 1994. This bear market was of similar magnitude to the others mentioned earlier that were not included.

Figure B.1, which shows a plot of index value relative to ten-year trend, has 1994 displayed as a prominent low, reflecting the sea change in stock returns that occurred at this point. The ten year trend was obtained by regression of log(index) versus time over the ten year period centered on the point of interest. Thus the trend for a point in 1990 is regression of data over 1985 to 1995. For points after 1997 or before 1807, the regression equation for the 1992-2002 and 1802-1812 period is used. This procedure is analogous to that used for GDP in Appendix A. None of the declines mentioned above feature prominently in Figure A.1. Thus, a bear market that produces a significant change in trend as shown in the figure, is also considered significant and should be considered in any list of important bear markets.

Figure B.1 Stock index versus its ten year trend, showing major bear market bottoms

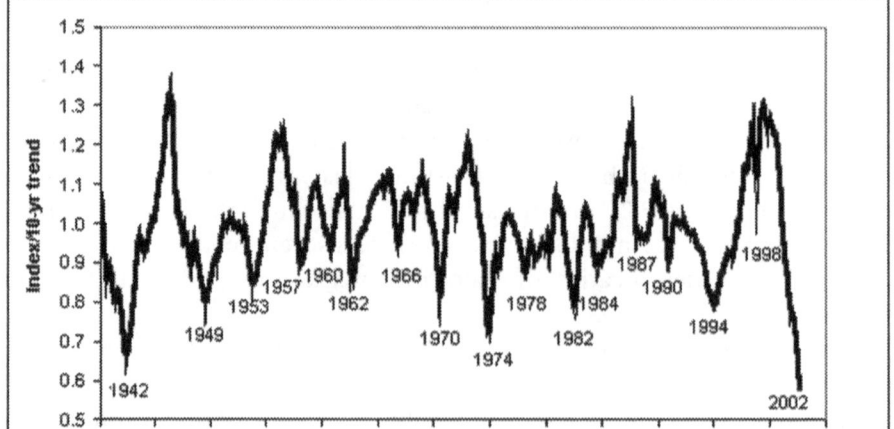

From these observations the following "rule" for bear markets was developed:

> A bear market is any decline of 20% or greater, or a severity of 0.5 or greater. Declines smaller than 20% and with severity between 0.1 and 0.5 are also considered bear markets if they occurred at the same time or just before an NBER recession, or form a major low on a plot of stock index versus 10-year trend.

Table B.1 shows all the bear markets by this definition since 1802. All of the bear markets listed by Bronson fall into these criteria. None of those I listed earlier do, and thus are not be included in the table.

There is one more issue with which I need to deal before a complete methodology for defining bear markets has been defined. One of Bronson's declines, the 1929 bear market, is part of a larger decline from 1929 to 1932—yet it is considered a separate bear market. Apparently, it seems the rally from Dow 195.4 on 11/13/29 to 297.3 on 4/16/30 was "big enough" to be considered a separate bull market. I can calculate a "severity" for this bull market as follows:

B.3   Bull market size = log (297.3/195.4) x 5.0 months = 0.91

A rally with severity of 0.9 or better, it would seem, constitutes a bull market. In comparison, I note the recent rally from S&P500 944.75 on September 21, 2001 to 1176.97 on January 7, 2002 scores an severity of only 0.34:

B.4   Bull market size = log (1176.97/944.75) x 3.6 months = 0.34

This is much smaller than the 1929-30 rally and is consistent with the general sense that the 2001-2002 rally was "just" another bear market rally and not a bull market.

The market nearly reached the January top on March 11, 2002. If I use this later date for the end of the rally I obtain a severity of 0.53, still well below the size of the 1929-30 rally. Nothing is changed. However, suppose the market had reached a peak of 1373 or higher on March 11, instead of forming a double top? In this case, the rally would have been as large as the 1929-1930 rise. Would such a large rally have been considered a bull market? It is impossible to know, but it seems reasonable to me that the vast majority of market participants would have hailed a rise of this magnitude (before it peaked) as a new bull market.

After this discussion one can add the definition of intervening bull market as a rise in a larger decline that is 0.9 or larger. This completes the rules for locating bear markets.

Table B.1. Bear markets since 1802

Top	Bottom	Severity	Rank	Top	Bottom	Severity	Rank
Dec 1802	Oct 1805	3.2	19	Nov 1919	Dec 1920	3.4	14
Dec 1809	Aug 1812	1.9	24	Mar 1923	Oct 1923	0.65	40
Dec 1813	Sep 1816	3.1	20	Feb 1926	Mar 1926[1]	0.12	53
June 1818	Jul 1819	0.9	38	Sep 1929	Nov 1929	0.66	39
Apr 1825	Jul 1829	3.4	16	Apr 1930	Jul 1932	22.8	1
Aug 1835	Jun 1837	4.0	12	Feb 1934	Jul 1934	0.63	42
Sep 1838	Jan 1843	10.2	3	Mar 1937	Mar 1938	3.7	13
Dec 1845	Jan 1848	0.9	37	Nov 1938	Apr 1942	9.3	4
Aug 1847	Nov 1848	1.7	28	May 1946	Oct 1946	0.63	43
Dec 1852	Jan 1855	3.4	17	Jun 1948	Jun 1949	1.45	30
Jul 1855	Oct 1857	7.8	7	Jan 1953	Sep 1953	0.58	46
Mar 1858	Jul 1859	1.4	31	Mar 1956	Oct 1957	1.87	25
Oct 1860	May 1861	0.9	36	Jan 1960	Oct 1960	0.61	44
Apr 1864	Jun 1865	1.8	26	Dec 1961	Jun 1962	0.97	34
Aug 1869	Dec 1869[1]	0.17	51	Feb 1966	Oct 1966	0.99	33
Feb 1873	Jun 1877	13.9	2	Dec 1968	May 1970	3.4	15
Jun 1881	Jan 1885	8.2	6	Jan 1973	Oct 1974	6.2	11
May 1887	Jun 1888	0.92	35	Sep 1976	Mar 1978	1.72	27
May 1890	Dec 1890	0.61	45	Feb 1980	Mar 1980[1]	0.15	52
Aug 1892	Aug 1893	1.7	29	Nov 1980	Aug 1982	2.82	23
Sep 1895	Aug 1896	1.12	32	Oct 1983	Jul 1984	0.65	41
Apr 1899	Sep 1900	2.9	21	Aug 1987	Oct 1987	0.35	48
Jun 1901	Nov 1903	7.7	8	Jul 1990	Oct 1990	0.28	50
Jan 1906	Nov 1907	6.3	10	Jan 1994	Dec 1994[2]	0.39	47
Nov 1909	Sep 1911	3.3	18	Jul 1998	Oct 1998	0.29	49
Sep 1912	Dec 1914	6.6	9	Mar 2000	Oct 2002	9.3	5
Nov 1916	Dec 1917	2.9	22				

[1] These bear markets are included only because they are associated with a recession.
[2] This bear market is included because it represents a major trend change (see Fig B.1)

Appendix C. Reduced Price

The idea behind reduced price is the simple quantity theory of money, expressed in differential form:

C.1 $\quad dP = V\, d(M/Y) = V\, dS$

Here P is the price level, M is the money supply, Y is real economic output and V is the velocity of money circulation, which is assumed to be constant. The quantity M/Y corresponds to what I have called stimulation (S). Integration of equation A.1 yields:

C.2 $\quad P = P_0 + V\, S$

Where P_0 is the value of P when S is zero. The idea behind this development is we don't have to know the exact level of S at the beginning of the inflationary periods. The constant term P_0 de-emphasizes the equilibrium period before the price inflation, for which we can observe the K-cycle directly by inspection. Instead, it places most emphasis on the period when S is rising strongly, which is exactly the period of interest.

Figure C.1. Reduced price calculated as P/S, 1960-present

One should be able to apply the quantity theory directly (i.e. equation C.2 with P_0 equal to zero). But this does not work well. Inclusion of a second parameter (P_0) is necessary to give a good fit of the price data. This is shown by the large value of P_0 relative to P for the nineteenth and early 20th century. For recent decades, P_0 has been small relative to P, suggesting that equation C.2 with P_0 equal to zero can be used:

C.3 $P = V S$ or $P/S = V$, $S = (M3 + \Sigma \text{ deficit})/GDP$

The advantage of this presentation is it can be calculated in real time (no regression is needed to obtain parameters). The ratio P/S was calculated for the period since 1960 using equation C.3 with monthly PPI for P, and monthly cumulative government deficit, M3 money supply and interpolated quarterly GDP for S. The results are shown in Figure C.1. The 1981 K-peak shows up clearly as does the post-1986 reduced price plateau. The figure shows that we almost fell off the plateau in 1998 in the aftermath of the long term capital management crisis and appear to be doing so today.

The expression given in equation C.3 and Figure C.1 is equivalent to the standard quantity theory of money and allows an interpretation of reduced price (P/S) as money velocity. This suggests that the K-cycle might be thought of as a velocity cycle.

Reduced price calculated according the equation C.3 was grafted onto reduced price calculated according to equation C.2 for the period after 1970 in Figure 4.1. The shape of the reduced price profile obtained with the regression method and equation 2 is the same. Both show the same dates for K-peak and the start of the plateau. Equation C.3 allows easier tracking of the developing fall from plateau (if this is indeed occurring).

Data Sources

The pre-1913 US producer price indices were obtained from Global Financial Data and Lebergott (1964). Post-1913 data was obtained from the Bureau of Labor Statistics. U.S. Money supply used in the construction of the stimulation variable (S) was M3 from 1959 to present and M2 from 1869 to 1959. M2 and M3 had almost identical values in 1959 so the two series were simply concatenated. Before 1869 the change in bank deposits was used to adjust the 1869 money supply level back to 1834. Before 1834 total currency was used to adjust money supply back to 1800. M3 was obtained from the Federal Reserve Bank of St. Louis, and pre-1959 M2 was obtained from the OSU Fisher college of business website. Bank deposits and currency were obtained by Mitchell (1998). Historical U.S. and U.K government deficits were obtained from Mitchell (1988, 1998). Recent U.S. economic data except deficits were obtained from economagic.com. Deficit data was obtained from the U.S. Department of Treasury monthly statement.

0-595-34206-X

www.ingramcontent.com/pod-product-compliance
Lightning Source LLC
Chambersburg PA
CBHW030800180526
45163CB00003B/1099